A Collection of Blog Posts

Partha Majumdar

A

C

Dedicated to

My niece, Bhavitha.

I hope this book kindles
her enthusiastic mind.

Preface

This collection combines a series of blog posts I've written over the years, reflecting on various aspects of life, work, philosophy, and society. From examining the origins of world religions to delving into the values of hard work and social justice, these pieces are inspired by my observations and the lessons I've gathered throughout my personal and professional journey.

As a professional deeply engaged in technology, business, and leadership, I have always sought to explore the intersection between the spiritual and the practical. This collection encapsulates my thoughts on how ancient wisdom informs modern challenges and how we, as individuals, can grow through knowledge and perseverance. Each essay offers a perspective shaped by my heritage, experiences, and passion for learning. These reflections will spark curiosity, inspire change, and serve as a source of contemplation.

I dedicate this collection to my niece, Bhavitha, hoping it kindles her curious and enthusiastic mind.

Partha Majumdar

C

d

Table of Contents

PREFACE.. **B**

THE ORIGINS OF MAJOR WORLD RELIGIONS 1

BUDDHISM: A REFORMATION FROM HINDUISM 4
The Buddha's Journey: A Departure from Vedic
Norms 4
Key Philosophical Distinctions between Buddhism
and Hinduism 6
Continuities with Hinduism 10
Buddhism's Global Influence....................... 11
JUDAISM: A JOURNEY TO LIBERATION 12
The Covenant with Abraham: The Birth of
Monotheism 12
Moses and the Exodus: A Defining Moment..... 14
The Torah: The Foundation of Jewish Law....... 15
The Importance of the Exodus in Jewish Identity
.... 16
Monotheism and the Concept of God in Judaism
.... 17
Prophets and Kings: The Evolution of Jewish Faith
.... 18
Judaism's Lasting Legacy 19
CHRISTIANITY: A FAITH BORN FROM OPPRESSION........ 21
The Life and Message of Jesus Christ 21
The Crucifixion and Resurrection 23
The Role of the Apostles: Spreading the Gospel24
The New Testament: A New Covenant 25
Separation from Judaism............................ 27
Persecution and Growth 28

The Triumph of Christianity in the Roman Empire 29

The Trinity and the Development of Christian Doctrine 30

ISLAM: A NEW REVELATION 32

The Early Life of Muhammad 32

Muhammad's First Revelation 33

The Message of Islam: Tawhid and Submission to God 34

The Quran: The Holy Book of Islam 36

Islam's Relationship with Judaism and Christianity 37

The Hijra: Migration to Medina and the Birth of the Islamic State 38

The Expansion of Islam: Challenges and Triumphs 39

The Caliphate and the Spread of Islam 40

The Legacy of Islam 41

SIKHISM: A SYNTHESIS OF HINDUISM AND ISLAM 43

The Life and Teachings of Guru Nanak 44

Key Beliefs of Sikhism 45

The Sikh Gurus: Shaping the Religion 47

The Formation of the Khalsa: Guru Gobind Singh's Legacy 50

Sikhism's Distinct Identity 52

HINDUISM: THE WORLD'S OLDEST RELIGION 54

The Origins of Hinduism: The Vedic Period 54

The Upanishads and the Rise of Philosophical Hinduism 56

The Epics and Puranas: Shaping Hindu History and Practice 58

9

Hindu Practices: Worship, Rituals, and the Pursuit of Moksha 60

Hindu Texts: A Wealth of Spiritual Wisdom 63

Diversity in Hinduism: Schools, Sects, and Philosophies 64

Philosophical Pluralism in Hinduism 66

Hinduism's Flexibility and Absorption of Cultural Influences 68

Hinduism in the Modern World 71

CONCLUSION 72

REFERENCES 74

COMPARING HINDUISM, BUDDHISM, AND SIKHISM **77**

DESCRIPTION OF HINDUISM, BUDDHISM, AND SIKHISM .. 78

SIMILARITIES 80

DIFFERENCES 81

CONCLUSION 83

REFERENCES 84

THE NUMBER 13: A SYMBOL OF SUPERSTITION, TRADITION, AND SPIRITUAL SIGNIFICANCE ..87

THE UNLUCKY NUMBER 13 IN THE WESTERN WORLD 87

THE SPIRITUAL SIGNIFICANCE OF 13 IN HINDUISM 89

THE ROLE OF 13 IN ISLAM 90

CONCLUSION 91

REFERENCES 92

WHY DO WE HAVE WARS? **95**

CREATION'S DUALITY: THE GOOD AND THE BAD 95

THE STRUGGLE BETWEEN GOOD AND BAD 96

DIVINE INTERVENTION TO RESTORE BALANCE 98

CONCLUSION 100

HARD WORK NEVER KILLS 103

HARD WORK IN THE INDIAN CONTEXT 103

INSIGHTS FROM THE RAMAYAN AND MAHABHARAT 105

AYURVEDIC PERSPECTIVE ON INDIVIDUAL CONSTITUTION

AND ENDURANCE...106

HARD WORK AND THE UNCERTAINTY OF LIFE 108

CONCLUSION 110

DO NOT PROCRASTINATE 113

WHEN A THOUGHT COMES TO MIND, NOTE IT DOWN AND

MARK THE TIME...113

START WORK ON THE THOUGHT AS QUICKLY AS POSSIBLE

....114

NOTE THE TIME WHEN THE THOUGHT WAS ACCOMPLISHED

....116

CELEBRATE EVERY ACCOMPLISHMENT, HOWEVER SMALL.118

GRADUALLY REDUCE THE TIME BETWEEN THE ARRIVAL OF

THOUGHTS AND THEIR ACCOMPLISHMENT 119

MAKE DECISIONS QUICKLY....................................119

THIS IS THE WAY TO LIVE IN THE PRESENT 121

THIS IS AN AGILE IMPLEMENTATION IN ONE'S PERSONAL

LIFE 122

CONCLUSION 123

THE DEMOCRATISATION OF EDUCATION IN INDIA: A LEAP FORWARD WITH ROOM FOR GROWTH 125

THE ONLINE EDUCATION WAVE.............................126

ECONOMIC BARRIERS TO ACCESS 126
IMPACT ON INNOVATION 127
THE ROLE OF CXOS AND POLICYMAKERS 128
CONCLUSION: A VISION FOR INCLUSIVE EDUCATION 129

**EMBRACING DATA ANALYTICS ACROSS
ORGANISATIONAL LEVELS: BEYOND THE C-
SUITE** **133**

REVOLUTIONISING RESOURCE OPTIMISATION 134
TRANSFORMING IT DEVELOPMENT AND MAINTENANCE ... 135
CONCLUSION 137

FOCUS ON THE STRENGTHS **141**

UNCOVERING INDIVIDUAL STRENGTHS 141
MAXIMISING POTENTIAL THROUGH STRENGTHS 142
CREATING SUPER TEAMS IN ORGANISATIONS 144
APPLYING THE PRINCIPLE IN SOCIAL LIFE 145
THE DETRIMENTAL IMPACT OF FOCUSING ON WEAKNESSES
.... 146
BUILDING A STRENGTH-BASED CULTURE 147
CONCLUSION 148

ABOUT THE AUTHOR .... **I**

BOOKS BY THE AUTHOR III

k

m

The Origins of Major World Religions

Religions have played an integral role in shaping civilisations, fostering cultures, and providing a moral compass to countless societies throughout history. Each major world religion has emerged from distinct historical, social, and spiritual contexts, reflecting how humans have sought meaning, purpose, and connection to the divine. The major world religions—Buddhism, Judaism, Christianity, Islam, Sikhism, and Hinduism—offer unique perspectives on the nature of existence, human suffering, the divine, and the ultimate purpose of life. They have guided civilisations through peace and conflict, influencing law, art, ethics, and human rights while addressing questions about mortality, justice, and salvation.

Understanding the origins and evolution of these religions sheds light on their profound impact on shaping the world's spiritual, philosophical, and social frameworks. While distinct in its core teachings and practices, each religion shares common threads of seeking truth, offering moral guidance, and fostering communal identity. These shared aspirations and their unique theological perspectives contribute to our vast religious diversity.

This article explores the foundational stories of these six major religions, analysing the conditions that led to their formation, their core teachings, and how they have transformed over time. Buddhism emerged as a reformation of Hinduism, critiquing the caste system and ritualism, while Judaism arose from a covenant between God and Abraham, offering the first major monotheistic worldview. Christianity evolved from a Jewish sect into a global religion based on the teachings of Jesus Christ. At the same time, Islam, born in the Arabian Peninsula, introduced a new revelation through Prophet Muhammad. Sikhism, drawing from both Hindu and Islamic elements, emerged as a distinct religion promoting equality and justice.

Hinduism, the world's oldest religion, developed over millennia through the absorption of diverse philosophical and spiritual influences.

By tracing these origins, this article aims to offer insights into the enduring influence of these religions, their role in shaping human history, and how they continue to guide the spiritual journeys of billions of people worldwide.

Buddhism: A Reformation from Hinduism

Buddhism, founded by Siddhartha Gautama (later known as the Buddha) around the 6th century BCE, arose during significant social and religious upheaval in India. Siddhartha was born into a noble family of the Shakya clan in Lumbini, in present-day Nepal. He was raised in the traditions of Hinduism, the predominant religious system of the time. This period saw a rigid caste system, with Brahmins (the priestly caste) exercising significant control over religious and social life. Rituals, sacrifices, and interpreting sacred texts (the Vedas) were largely confined to the Brahmin class, leading to social stratification and exclusion.

The Buddha's Journey: A Departure from Vedic Norms

Siddhartha's early life was one of luxury. Still, his eventual exposure to the realities of human suffering—old age, sickness, and death—prompted him to seek answers beyond the rituals and caste restrictions of the Vedic tradition. He renounced his princely life in search of spiritual liberation and enlightenment. After years of asceticism and meditation, he attained *Nirvana* (spiritual enlightenment) under the Bodhi tree in Bodh Gaya.

Buddhism's origin partly critiqued certain aspects of Hindu society, particularly the caste system and the Brahminical monopoly on religious practices. While Siddhartha retained several core philosophical elements from the Vedic tradition—such as *karma* (the law of moral causation), *dharma* (ethical duty), and *samsara* (the cycle of rebirth)—his teachings presented a significant departure from the Hindu concepts of *Brahman* (the ultimate, formless reality) and *atman* (the soul or self).

Key Philosophical Distinctions between Buddhism and Hinduism

1. **Caste System**: Hindu society was (and still is, in some ways) stratified into four main castes—Brahmins, Kshatriyas, Vaishyas, and Shudras. Each caste had specific duties and responsibilities, with the Brahmins occupying the highest position in religious matters. Troubled by the inequalities perpetuated by this system, Siddhartha advocated for a casteless society where all individuals could work toward their spiritual liberation, regardless of birth status. Buddhism, therefore, promotes *sangha* (community) based on spiritual merit rather than social class.

2. **No Supreme Creator God**: While Hinduism espouses belief in *Brahman*—a formless, infinite, and eternal supreme reality that manifests in various deities—Buddhism does not affirm the existence of a creator god.

The Buddha refrained from theological debates about the divine, focusing instead on the practical path to end human suffering through self-effort and wisdom. The Buddha's teachings emphasised a *nontheistic* approach to spirituality, where individuals are responsible for their liberation (through the Eightfold Path) rather than relying on divine intervention.

3. **No Permanent Self (Anatta)**: One of Buddhism's most revolutionary ideas is the doctrine of *anatta* (non-self), which challenges the Hindu concept of *atman* (the soul or eternal self). While Hinduism holds that the *atman* is the true essence of an individual, infinite and unchanging, Buddhism teaches that there is no permanent self. According to the Buddha, what we perceive as the self is merely a collection of ever-changing physical and mental components (the five aggregates: form, sensation, perception, mental formations, and consciousness). This

impermanence is a core cause of suffering (*dukkha*), and understanding the absence of a permanent self is essential to attaining Nirvana.

4. **Rejection of Vedic Rituals and Priestly Authority**: At the time of Siddhartha, Hinduism was dominated by elaborate Vedic rituals and sacrifices, often led by Brahmin priests. These rituals were necessary for maintaining cosmic order and achieving worldly success or spiritual rewards. The Buddha, however, rejected the idea that rituals or intermediaries were essential for spiritual progress. His teachings emphasised personal ethical conduct, meditation, and direct insight into the nature of reality as the means to enlightenment.

5. **The Four Noble Truths and the Eightfold Path**: Central to the Buddha's teachings are the Four Noble Truths:

- **The truth of suffering (*dukkha*)**: All beings experience suffering in various forms.
- **The truth of the cause of suffering (*samudaya*)**: The root of suffering lies in attachment, craving, and ignorance.
- **The truth of the cessation of suffering (*nirodha*)**: It is possible to end suffering by eliminating its causes.
- **The truth of the path to the cessation of suffering (*magga*)**: The Eightfold Path achieves this end.

The Eightfold Path includes right understanding, right intention, right speech, right action, right livelihood, right effort, right mindfulness, and right concentration. This ethical and philosophical guide forms the core of Buddhist practice, offering a middle way between self-indulgence and extreme asceticism.

Continuities with Hinduism

Despite its departure from Hindu orthodoxy, Buddhism remains deeply connected to many aspects of the Indian spiritual tradition.

- **Karma and Rebirth**: Buddhism and Hinduism hold that one's actions (*karma*) determine future experiences, whether in this life or the next. Both religions also accept the concept of *samsara*, the cycle of birth, death, and rebirth.
- **Meditative   Practices**: Meditation, a central Buddhist practice, was already prevalent in certain Vedic traditions. Through his insights, the Buddha developed specific meditation techniques (such as *vipassana* or insight meditation) to cultivate mindfulness and wisdom.

Buddhism's Global Influence

Over time, Buddhism spread beyond India, becoming a major spiritual force in Central, East, and Southeast Asia. While it gradually declined in India, its birthplace, it flourished in countries like Sri Lanka, China, Japan, Korea, and Tibet. Each region developed its interpretation of the Buddha's teachings, leading to the formation of distinct schools, such as Theravada (The School of the Elders), Mahayana (The Great Vehicle), and Vajrayana (The Diamond Vehicle).

Judaism: A Journey to Liberation

Often regarded as the world's first major monotheistic religion, Judaism traces its origins to the ancient Near East over 4,000 years ago. The narrative begins with the patriarch Abraham, considered the father of the Jewish people, and his covenant with God (*Yahweh*). This foundational moment is believed to have occurred around 2000 BCE. However, Judaism's most formative story centres on Moses and the Exodus from Egypt, an event defining the Jewish people's identity and covenantal relationship with God.

The Covenant with Abraham: The Birth of Monotheism

The story of Judaism begins with Abraham, who lived in the ancient city of Ur in Mesopotamia (modern-day Iraq). According to Jewish tradition, God called Abraham to leave his homeland and travel to Canaan (modern-day Israel/Palestine), where he would become the father of a great nation. This covenant, or sacred agreement, established Abraham and his descendants as God's chosen people, tasked with upholding His commandments and spreading the knowledge of the one true God.

The covenant between God and Abraham significantly departs from the polytheistic beliefs that dominated the ancient world. Unlike the gods of Mesopotamia, Egypt, and other ancient civilisations, the God of Abraham was singular, omnipotent, omniscient, and deeply involved in His people's moral and ethical lives. This monotheism would become the cornerstone of the Jewish faith.

The covenant also promised that Abraham's descendants would inherit the land of Canaan and that through them, all nations of the world would be blessed. Abraham's faith and obedience are the foundation of the Jewish people's enduring relationship with God, often called the Abrahamic Covenant.

Moses and the Exodus: A Defining Moment

While Abraham's covenant established the Jewish people's unique relationship with God, the story of Moses and the Exodus solidified their identity as a nation. The Exodus is considered one of the most important narratives in Judaism, recounting the Israelites' escape from slavery in Egypt and their journey toward the Promised Land.

The Israelites had settled in Egypt during a famine, but as their numbers grew, they were eventually enslaved by the Egyptians. According to the Hebrew Bible (the *Tanakh*), Moses, born to an Israelite family but raised as a prince in the Egyptian court, was chosen by God to lead his people to freedom. After several miraculous plagues inflicted on Egypt, Pharaoh finally agreed to let the Israelites go.

The journey from Egypt, however, was challenging. The Israelites wandered in the desert for 40 years before reaching the Promised Land of Canaan. Along the way, Moses received the Ten Commandments from

God at Mount Sinai, a momentous event that provided Judaism's moral and legal foundation. The Ten Commandments form the core of Jewish law, known as the *Torah*.

The Torah: The Foundation of Jewish Law

The Torah, often translated as "instruction" or "law," is the central text of Judaism. It consists of the first five books of the Hebrew Bible—*Genesis, Exodus, Leviticus, Numbers,* and *Deuteronomy*—and outlines the laws and teachings that guide Jewish life. While the Ten Commandments are the most well-known part of the Torah, 613 *mitzvot* (commandments) govern every aspect of life, from ethical behaviour to religious rituals.

At the heart of the Torah is a covenantal relationship between God and the Jewish people. God is not a distant, indifferent deity but one who cares deeply about justice, morality, and the well-being of His creation. In return, the Jewish people are expected to live according to God's laws, promoting righteousness and justice in the world.

The Torah emphasises the importance of ethical monotheism—the belief that God is one and demands ethical behaviour from His people. This ethical framework sets Judaism apart from many ancient religions, which often focused on ritual sacrifices and appeasing the gods rather than moral conduct.

The Importance of the Exodus in Jewish Identity

The Exodus story is central to Jewish religious and cultural identity. It is commemorated annually during the festival of Passover (*Pesach*), which celebrates the Israelites' liberation from Egyptian bondage. The story of the Exodus is not just a historical event but also a powerful symbol of hope, resilience, and divine justice. Throughout Jewish history, the Exodus has been a source of inspiration during times of persecution, exile, and hardship.

The Exodus's liberation, justice, and covenant themes resonate in Jewish thought and practice. The belief that God intervenes in history to save His people from oppression has shaped Jewish understanding of their relationship with God and their mission in the world.

Monotheism and the Concept of God in Judaism

Judaism's revolutionary contribution to religious thought is its concept of monotheism—the belief in one, all-powerful, and indivisible God. This contrasts sharply with the polytheistic traditions of surrounding cultures, where gods were often associated with natural forces, cities, or specific peoples. In Judaism, God is the creator of the entire universe and is not limited to any geographical region or people.

Judaism also introduces the idea that God is both transcendent and immanent. He is above and beyond the physical world yet intimately involved in human affairs, guiding and shaping history. This belief is reflected in the Jewish prayer *Shema Yisrael* ("Hear, O Israel: the Lord our God, the Lord is one"), which affirms God's unity and uniqueness.

God's relationship with humanity is not one of fear or appeasement but one of love and justice. The Jewish understanding of God is deeply ethical; He is a God who demands justice, righteousness, and compassion. This ethical monotheism profoundly influenced the development of Western religious and moral thought.

Prophets and Kings: The Evolution of Jewish Faith

After the Exodus and the entry into the Promised Land, the Israelites established a kingdom under leaders like King David and Solomon. During this period, prophets were crucial in guiding and reminding the people of their covenantal obligations. Figures like Isaiah, Jeremiah, and Ezekiel called for social justice, repentance, and faithfulness to God's commandments.

The destruction of the First Temple by the Babylonians in 586 BCE and the subsequent exile of the Jewish people to Babylon were traumatic events that reshaped Jewish theology. In exile, the Jewish people deepened their commitment to the Torah and the covenant, preserving their identity despite losing their homeland.

Judaism's Lasting Legacy

Judaism's contribution to world history is immeasurable. Its monotheistic belief system laid the groundwork for Christianity and Islam, two other major world religions with the same Abrahamic roots. Judaism's ethical teachings, particularly its emphasis on justice, compassion, and the sanctity of human life have deeply influenced Western moral and legal thought.

Despite centuries of persecution and diaspora, the Jewish people have maintained their faith, culture, and traditions, remaining one of the oldest continuous religious communities in the world. Judaism's rich theological and legal traditions, its profound sense of history, and its unshakable faith in God's covenant with His people continue to inspire millions today.

Christianity: A Faith Born from Oppression

Christianity, one of the largest religions in the world today, originated in the 1st century CE in the Roman province of Judea (modern-day Israel/Palestine). The region was under Roman rule, and the Jewish population lived under harsh economic and political oppression. Within this context, Christianity arose as a movement within Judaism centred around the teachings of Jesus of Nazareth, a Jewish preacher who challenged religious authorities and Roman rule, preaching a radical message of love, forgiveness, and salvation.

The Life and Message of Jesus Christ

Jesus was born into a Jewish family, likely around 4 BCE, during the reign of King Herod the Great. His teachings, recorded in the Gospels, emphasised the coming of the Kingdom of God, a new age of justice and peace where God's will would be fully realised. He called for repentance, faith in God, and the practice of unconditional love and forgiveness toward others. These teachings struck a chord with the common people but also brought him into conflict with the Jewish religious authorities, particularly the Pharisees and Sadducees, and with Roman rulers, who saw his growing influence as a threat to their control.

One of the central aspects of Jesus' message was the idea of personal salvation and redemption through faith in God. He taught that God's love extended to all people, including the marginalised, sinners, and outcasts. He also spoke of eternal life, promising those who believed in him would enter the Kingdom of Heaven. These concepts of universal love, mercy, and salvation were revolutionary and challenged the religious practices of the time, which were often seen as legalistic and exclusive.

The Crucifixion and Resurrection

The tension between Jesus and the authorities culminated in his arrest and crucifixion, an event central to Christian belief. According to Christian doctrine, Jesus' crucifixion was not the end but a necessary sacrifice for the sins of humanity. Christians believe that three days after his death, Jesus rose from the dead—a belief known as the Resurrection. This event, as described in the Gospels, is considered the foundation of the Christian faith. It confirmed Jesus as the Messiah (the "Christ" in Greek), and his resurrection symbolised hope, victory over death, and the promise of eternal life for all believers.

The crucifixion and resurrection gave rise to the Christian belief in Jesus as the *Son of God* and the *Savior of humanity*, who had fulfilled the messianic prophecies of the Hebrew Bible (Old Testament). The resurrection solidified the faith of Jesus' followers and set the stage for the spread of Christianity throughout the Roman Empire.

The Role of the Apostles: Spreading the Gospel

After Jesus' death and resurrection, his followers, known as apostles, began to spread his teachings. Central figures in this early Christian movement included Peter, traditionally regarded as the apostles' leader, and Paul, a former Pharisee who experienced a profound conversion and became one of Christianity's most influential missionaries.

- **Peter**: One of Jesus' closest disciples, Peter is often considered the first leader of the Christian community in Jerusalem. According to tradition, he was instrumental in spreading the message of Jesus among Jewish communities.
- **Paul**: Originally known as Saul of Tarsus, Paul was a devout Jew and a Roman citizen who initially persecuted Christians. After a dramatic vision of the risen Jesus on the road to Damascus, Paul became one of Christianity's most fervent advocates. His missionary journeys across the Roman Empire

helped spread the faith to non-Jewish (Gentile) communities, particularly in cities like Corinth, Ephesus, and Rome. Paul's letters (epistles) to these early Christian communities form a significant portion of the New Testament.

The apostles emphasised Jesus' message of salvation and the belief that his death and resurrection offered redemption from sin. They travelled extensively, founding Christian communities and preaching that faith in Jesus was the path to eternal life. This missionary zeal and relative ease of travel within the Roman Empire allowed Christianity to spread rapidly beyond its Jewish roots.

The New Testament: A New Covenant

The New Testament, written by the apostles and early followers of Jesus, provides the theological and historical foundation of

Christianity. While it builds on the Jewish *Tanakh* (referred to by Christians as the Old Testament), the New Testament introduces new theological concepts, such as the belief in the Trinity (Father, Son, and Holy Spirit) and the idea of a New Covenant between God and humanity, fulfilled through Jesus' life, death, and resurrection.

The New Testament consists of:

1. The Gospels (Matthew, Mark, Luke, and John) narrate Jesus's life, teachings, death, and resurrection.
2. The Acts of the Apostles detail the early Christian community and the spread of the faith after Jesus' ascension.
3. The Epistles are letters Paul and other apostles wrote to various Christian communities, offering theological guidance and moral teachings.
4. The Book of Revelation is a prophetic text that speaks of

God's ultimate victory over evil and establishing a new heaven and earth.

Through these writings, Christianity preserved Jesus' teachings and developed new theological doctrines, particularly concerning salvation, grace, and the role of the Church.

Separation from Judaism

Christianity initially emerged as a Jewish sect. Jesus and his earliest followers were Jews who followed Jewish law and traditions. However, as Christianity spread among Gentile populations, particularly through the efforts of Paul, it gradually separated from its Jewish roots. One key point of division was whether Gentile converts needed to observe Jewish laws, such as circumcision and dietary restrictions. Paul argued that faith in Christ alone was sufficient for salvation and that adherence to Jewish law was no longer necessary.

This theological shift, along with increasing hostility from both Jewish and Roman authorities, led to a gradual estrangement between Christians and Jews. By the end of the 1st century CE, Christianity had developed into a distinct religion with its beliefs, practices, and community structures.

Persecution and Growth

For the first three centuries, Christianity was a minority religion often persecuted by the Roman authorities. Christians refused to participate in worshipping Roman gods and the emperor, which was seen as a threat to the stability of the Roman state. Many Christians were martyred for their faith during this period, and their courage and steadfastness in the face of persecution helped to strengthen and spread the movement.

Despite these challenges, Christianity grew, attracting converts from diverse backgrounds, including Jews and Gentiles. The message of hope, salvation, and eternal life resonated with many people living under Roman rule, particularly those marginalised by society.

The Triumph of Christianity in the Roman Empire

In the early 4th century, Christianity transformed dramatically from a persecuted faith to the dominant religion of the Roman Empire. This shift began with the conversion of Emperor Constantine the Great, who, after reportedly seeing a vision of the cross before a crucial battle, embraced Christianity and issued the Edict of Milan in 313 CE, granting religious tolerance to Christians.

Constantine's conversion and support for Christianity paved the way for spreading the faith throughout the empire. By the end of the 4th century, under Emperor Theodosius I, Christianity was declared the Roman Empire's official religion, marking a monumental turning point in its history.

The Trinity and the Development of Christian Doctrine

One of the most distinctive theological developments in Christianity is the doctrine of the Trinity, which describes God as one being in three persons: the Father, the Son (Jesus Christ), and the Holy Spirit. While this concept is not explicitly outlined in the New Testament, it was developed by early Christian theologians in response to debates about the nature of Jesus and his relationship with God.

The Council of Nicaea, convened by Constantine in 325 CE, was a landmark event in developing Christian doctrine. At this council, the Nicene Creed was formulated, affirming the belief in the Trinity and declaring that Jesus was of the same substance (*homoousios*) as God the Father. This

countered the Arian heresy, which claimed
that Jesus was a created being.

Islam: A New Revelation

Islam, one of the world's major monotheistic religions, was founded in the 7th century CE by the Prophet Muhammad in Mecca, located in present-day Saudi Arabia. During social, political, and spiritual turmoil, Islam emerged in a region of diverse religious beliefs, including polytheism, Christianity, Judaism, and Zoroastrianism. The Arabian Peninsula was a trade centre, and Mecca was an important religious site, with the Kaaba, a sanctuary housing numerous deities worshipped by the local tribes.

Muhammad's prophetic mission began within this context, forming a new religious and political community that would profoundly influence world history.

The Early Life of Muhammad

Muhammad was born around 570 CE into the Quraysh tribe, the ruling tribe of Mecca. He was orphaned at a young age and was raised by his uncle, Abu Talib. Growing up,

Muhammad gained a reputation for his honesty and trustworthiness, earning him the nickname *Al-Amin* (the trustworthy). As a young man, he worked as a merchant, and through his trade, he met Jews, Christians, and other religious groups, which likely influenced his spiritual development.

At 25, Muhammad married Khadija, a wealthy widow who supported him throughout the early years of his prophetic mission. Despite his success as a merchant, Muhammad was deeply troubled by the social inequalities, tribal conflicts, and moral decay he witnessed in Meccan society. He often retreated to the cave of Hira in the mountains surrounding Mecca to meditate and seek spiritual guidance.

Muhammad's First Revelation

At 40, during one of these retreats, Muhammad received his first revelation from the angel Gabriel (*Jibril* in Arabic). This event, known as the *Laylat al-Qadr* (the Night of Power), marked the beginning of

Muhammad's prophetic career. Gabriel revealed to Muhammad the words of God, which he was instructed to recite. These revelations continued for the next 23 years of Muhammad's life, forming the basis of the Quran, Islam's holy book.

The first revealed verses emphasised the oneness of God (*Allah*) and called on Muhammad to spread the message of monotheism, righteousness, and social justice. Muhammad's message challenged the polytheistic practices of the Quraysh, who were deeply invested in idol worship centred around the Kaaba.

The Message of Islam: Tawhid and Submission to God

At the heart of Islam is the concept of *tawhid*, or the absolute oneness of God. Islam teaches that God is the sole creator and sustainer of the universe and merciful, all-knowing, and all-powerful. The term "Islam" itself means "submission" or "surrender" to the will of God, and a Muslim submits to God's divine will.

Muhammad's early teachings focused on recognising God's unity and living a life of moral integrity, justice, and compassion. Islam also introduced the concept of the *umma*, or the global Muslim community, united by faith in the one God. The *Five Pillars of Islam* are key to Islamic belief, which outline the essential acts of worship and devotion that every Muslim must follow.

1. **Shahada** (Faith): The declaration of faith, stating that there is no god but God (*Allah*) and Muhammad is His messenger.
2. **Salat** (Prayer): The performance of five daily prayers facing Mecca.
3. **Zakat** (Charity): Giving alms to the poor and needy, emphasising social justice and the equitable distribution of wealth.
4. **Sawm** (Fasting): Observing the fast during Ramadan, a time of self-discipline and reflection.

5. **Hajj** (Pilgrimage): The pilgrimage to Mecca, which every Muslim must undertake at least once in their lifetime if able.

These pillars define Islam's spiritual practices and emphasise the importance of community, charity, and submission to God's will.

The Quran: The Holy Book of Islam

The Quran, regarded by Muslims as the literal word of God, was revealed to Muhammad over 23 years ago and compiled into its current form shortly after his death. It is the ultimate guide for Muslims, providing instructions on faith, morality, law, and personal conduct. It addresses various topics, from God's nature and the universe's creation to family life, social justice, and governance.

Unlike the Jewish and Christian scriptures, which evolved over centuries, the Quran is believed to be the unaltered and final revelation of God's will, preserved in its original Arabic form. Muslims consider it the definitive and complete guide for human life, superseding earlier revelations from prophets like Abraham, Moses, and Jesus.

Islam's Relationship with Judaism and Christianity

Islam shares many foundational beliefs and stories with Judaism and Christianity. Muslims revere figures such as Abraham (*Ibrahim*), Moses (*Musa*), and Jesus (*Isa*) as prophets who conveyed God's message to humanity. Islam regards itself as the continuation and completion of the monotheistic tradition, with Muhammad as the final prophet (*Khatam an-Nabiyyin*), bringing God's ultimate and most complete revelation.

While Islam acknowledges the importance of the Torah and the Gospels, Muslims believe that these earlier scriptures were altered or misunderstood over time. The Quran, therefore, is seen as the correction and completion of God's guidance, restoring the true message of monotheism. In Islamic theology, both Jews and Christians are considered "People of the Book" (*Ahl al-Kitab*), and they are accorded a special status in Islamic law, though their scriptures are seen as incomplete.

The Hijra: Migration to Medina and the Birth of the Islamic State

As Muhammad's message gained followers in Mecca, it also attracted increasing hostility from the Quraysh, who saw his monotheistic preaching as a threat to their political and economic interests. In 622 CE, facing persecution, Muhammad and his followers fled to the city of Yathrib (later renamed Medina), an event known as the *Hijra*. This migration marks the beginning of the Islamic calendar and the establishment of the first

Muslim community under Muhammad's leadership.

Muhammad acted as a spiritual, political, and military leader in Medina. He established the Constitution of Medina, which created a framework for peaceful coexistence among the city's diverse population, including Muslims, Jews, and pagan tribes. This document is one of the earliest examples of a pluralistic society governed by Islamic principles of justice and fairness.

The Expansion of Islam: Challenges and Triumphs

In the years following the Hijra, Islam rapidly expanded throughout the Arabian Peninsula. Muhammad and his followers faced several military challenges, including conflicts with the Quraysh and other tribes. Notable battles, such as the Battle of Badr and the Battle of Uhud, played a significant role in consolidating Muslim power.

In 630 CE, Muhammad and his followers returned to Mecca and peacefully conquered the city. Upon entering the Kaaba, Muhammad cleansed it of its idols and rededicated it to worship the one true God, Allah. This act symbolised the triumph of monotheism over polytheism in Arabia.

By Muhammad's death in 632 CE, Islam had spread throughout most of the Arabian Peninsula, and its influence was beginning to extend beyond. The rapid expansion of Islam in the decades following Muhammad's death can be attributed to a combination of factors, including the appeal of its message, the administrative and military prowess of early Muslim leaders, and the political instability of the neighbouring Byzantine and Sassanian empires.

The Caliphate and the Spread of Islam

After Muhammad's death, the Muslim community faced the challenge of succession.

The title of *caliph* (successor) was given to Abu Bakr, one of Muhammad's closest companions, and under his leadership, the caliphate expanded beyond the Arabian Peninsula. The early caliphs, known as the *Rashidun* (rightly guided) caliphs, continued to spread Islam through conquest and diplomacy, extending Muslim rule into the Levant, Persia, Egypt, and North Africa.

The spread of Islam was not merely a result of military conquests; it was also facilitated by trade, missionary efforts, and the appeal of its message of equality and justice. Many regions under Muslim rule, particularly in North Africa and the Middle East, gradually converted to Islam over the centuries, drawn by its emphasis on social justice, the equality of all believers, and the simplicity of its monotheistic creed.

The Legacy of Islam

One of the most remarkable phenomena in history is Islam's rapid rise from a small religious movement in 7th-century Arabia to a major world religion within a century. Today, Islam is the second-largest religion in the world, with over 1.8 billion followers. Its teachings continue to shape the lives of millions of people, influencing religious practices, law, culture, and politics in Muslim-majority societies.

Central to Islam's lasting influence is its ability to adapt to diverse cultural contexts while maintaining its core message of *tawhid* (the oneness of God) and *submission to God's will*. As the final revelation, the Quran remains the guiding text for Muslims, offering spiritual, moral, and legal guidance for individuals and communities.

Sikhism: A Synthesis of Hinduism and Islam

Sikhism, one of the youngest major world religions, was founded in the late 15th century in the Punjab region of India by Guru Nanak. Its emergence occurred in a period marked by social, religious, and political strife. The area, then under the rule of the Mughal Empire, witnessed tensions between the Hindu majority and the ruling Muslim elite, each practising distinct religious traditions. In this context, Guru Nanak's teachings offered a new spiritual path, promoting devotion to one God, equality, and the rejection of rigid social hierarchies and rituals.

Sikhism developed as a distinct religion that drew on elements from both Hindu and Islamic traditions but ultimately forged a unique identity. Over time, the teachings of Guru Nanak were consolidated and expanded by subsequent Sikh Gurus, most notably Guru Gobind Singh, who established the Khalsa, the community of committed Sikhs, and institutionalised the faith.

The Life and Teachings of Guru Nanak

Guru Nanak, the founder of Sikhism, was born in 1469 CE in a small village called Talwandi (now Nankana Sahib in modern-day Pakistan). From a young age, Nanak demonstrated a deep spiritual inclination, questioning the prevailing religious practices and social injustices around him. He rejected the ritualism and formalism in Hinduism and Islam and sought a direct connection with the divine.

At 30, Guru Nanak experienced a profound spiritual revelation, after which he began travelling across India and beyond, spreading his message. His teachings focused on the oneness of God (*Ik Onkar*), the equality of all human beings, and the importance of leading a life of truth, compassion, and humility. He emphasised that true spirituality lay not in religious rituals but in devotion to God, ethical conduct, and service to others.

One of Guru Nanak's key messages was rejecting the caste system, which had become deeply entrenched in Hindu society. He preached that all humans are equal in the eyes of God, regardless of their caste, creed, or gender. This belief in social equality was revolutionary then and became a core tenet of Sikhism.

Key Beliefs of Sikhism

Sikhism is a monotheistic faith that believes in one, formless, and all-pervading God. The primary scripture of Sikhism, the *Guru Granth Sahib*, emphasises devotion to God, righteous living, and pursuing spiritual wisdom. Some of the core beliefs and principles of Sikhism include the following.

1. **Oneness of God** (*Ik Onkar*): Sikhism teaches that only one God is the same for all people, regardless of their religion or background. This God is formless, timeless, transcendent, and immanent, present in all creation.

2. **Equality and Social Justice**: Guru Nanak rejected the hierarchical structures of caste, class, and gender. He taught everyone to be treated with respect and dignity regardless of social status. Sikhism advocates for social justice and the fair treatment of all individuals.

3. **Rejection of Ritualism**: Sikhism is critical of empty rituals and superstitions found in both Hinduism and Islam. Guru Nanak emphasised inner devotion, ethical living, and remembrance of God through meditation (*Naam Simran*) rather than ritualistic practices.

4. **The Three Pillars of Sikhism**: Guru Nanak's teachings revolve around three central practices.
   - ***Naam Japna***: Meditating on God's name.

- **_Kirat Karni_**: Earning an honest living through hard work and righteous means.
- **_Vand Chakna_**: Sharing with others, especially those in need, and practising charity.

5. **The Importance of Community Service (Seva)**: Sikhs are encouraged to engage in selfless service to the community, reflecting the importance of humility and compassion in their faith. This principle is embodied in the practice of Langar, the community kitchen where free meals are served to people of all backgrounds, a practice started by Guru Nanak.

The Sikh Gurus: Shaping the Religion

After Guru Nanak died in 1539, his spiritual and leadership role was passed on to nine successive Gurus, each of whom contributed to the growth and development of Sikhism. These Gurus guided the Sikh community and elaborated on Guru Nanak's teachings.

- **Guru Angad (1504–1552)**: The second Guru, Guru Angad, institutionalised the *Gurmukhi* script, which became the standard for writing the Punjabi language. This helped preserve the teachings of Guru Nanak in written form.
- **Guru Amar Das (1479–1574)**: The third Guru emphasised social equality, particularly women's rights. He established *Manji* and *Piri*, systems of community governance that empowered women to lead religious gatherings.
- **Guru Ram Das (1534–1581)**: The fourth Guru founded the city of Amritsar, which became the spiritual and cultural centre of Sikhism.

- **Guru Arjan (1563–1606)**: The fifth Guru compiled the *Adi Granth*, the precursor to the *Guru Granth Sahib*, and oversaw the construction of the Harmandir Sahib (Golden Temple) in Amritsar, the holiest shrine in Sikhism. Guru Arjan was executed by Mughal authorities, marking the beginning of Sikh persecution under Mughal rule.
- **Guru Hargobind (1595–1644)**: The sixth Guru adopted a more militant stance in response to Mughal aggression. He emphasised the importance of defending the faith and introduced the concept of *Miri* and *Piri*, symbolised by two swords, representing temporal and spiritual authority.
- **Guru Tegh Bahadur (1621–1675)**: The ninth Guru is remembered for his martyrdom defending religious freedom. He

was executed by Mughal Emperor Aurangzeb for resisting forced conversions of Hindus to Islam, further solidifying Sikhism's stance against religious persecution.

The Formation of the Khalsa: Guru Gobind Singh's Legacy

Guru Gobind Singh, the tenth and final human Guru, played a pivotal role in shaping Sikhism as it exists today. Born in 1666, Guru Gobind Singh faced increasing persecution from the Mughal authorities. In response to these challenges, he established the *Khalsa* in 1699, a community of initiated Sikhs who were committed to defending their faith and living by the highest moral standards.

The Khalsa was created during the festival of *Vaisakhi* when Guru Gobind Singh called on Sikhs to come forward and offer their lives for their faith. Five Sikhs stepped forward, and they became the first members of the Khalsa, known as the *Panj Pyare* (the Five Beloved Ones). They were initiated through a ceremony involving the preparation and drinking of *Amrit* (sugar water), symbolising spiritual rebirth.

The creation of the Khalsa transformed Sikhism into a more organised and militant community, ready to defend itself against external threats. Members of the Khalsa were given a distinct identity, marked by the *Five Ks*.

1. **Kesh**: Uncut hair, symbolising spirituality and respect for God's creation.
2. **Kanga**: A wooden comb representing cleanliness and discipline.
3. **Kara**: A steel bracelet that signifies unity with God and the Sikh community.
4. **Kachera**: Cotton undergarments symbolising modesty and self-control.

5. **Kirpan**: A ceremonial sword representing the Sikh's duty to protect the weak and uphold justice.

In addition to founding the Khalsa, Guru Gobind Singh declared that after his death, the Sikh community would no longer have a human Guru. Instead, the *Guru Granth Sahib*, the Sikh holy scripture, would serve as the eternal Guru, and the Khalsa would act as the temporal and spiritual leader of the Sikh people.

Sikhism's Distinct Identity

While Sikhism incorporates elements from Hinduism and Islam, it is a distinct religion with its own theological, ethical, and social framework. Unlike Hinduism, Sikhism rejects the caste system and idol worship. Unlike Islam, Sikhism does not practice circumcision or endorse a fixed legal code like Sharia. Instead, Sikhism offers a spiritual path focused on worshipping one formless God, ethical living, and pursuing justice and equality.

The unique blend of Hindu and Islamic elements, combined with the leadership of the Sikh Gurus, shaped Sikhism into a distinct faith that promotes a just and egalitarian society. Its emphasis on the oneness of God, rejection of social hierarchies, and dedication to community service set it apart as a religion that advocates both spiritual and social transformation.

Hinduism: The World's Oldest Religion

Unlike the other major world religions, Hinduism has no single founder or specific moment of origin. Instead, it is a vast, diverse, and evolving religious tradition developed over millennia in the Indian subcontinent. It is often described as *Sanatana Dharma*, meaning "the eternal way" or "the eternal order," reflecting its spiritual teachings' timeless and enduring nature. Hinduism is the oldest living religion, with roots stretching over 9,000 years, making it one of the world's most ancient belief systems.

The Origins of Hinduism: The Vedic Period

The earliest roots of Hinduism can be traced to the Vedic period, which began around 9000 years ago. During this time, the sacred texts known as the Vedas were composed, marking the beginning of Hindu thought. The Vedas—

Rigveda,   Samaveda,   Yajurveda,   and
Atharvaveda—are   considered   the
foundational   texts   of   Hinduism   and   are
regarded as *Shrutis* ("that which is heard"),
believed   to   have   been   divinely   revealed   to
ancient sages, known as *rishis*.

The Vedas contain hymns, prayers, rituals,
and   philosophical   discussions   centred   on
cosmology,   nature,   and   the   nature   of
existence. The primary focus of early Vedic
religion was the worship of natural forces and
deities, such as *Agni* (fire), *Indra* (the king of
the gods), and *Surya* (the sun). These deities
were   invoked   through   complex   rituals   and
sacrifices   (*yajna*)   conducted   by   priests
(*Brahmins*),   who   played   a   crucial   role   in
mediating between humans and the divine.

Over   time,   the   Vedic   tradition   gave   rise   to
various philosophical and religious ideas that
became   integral   to   Hinduism.   As   the   Vedic
corpus   expanded,   so   did   its   interpretations,
leading   to   multiple   schools   of   thought   and
practices.

The Upanishads and the Rise of Philosophical Hinduism

Around 800-500 BCE, a body of spiritual texts known as the Upanishads emerged. These texts represent the philosophical culmination of the Vedic tradition and mark a shift from ritualistic worship to reflective and meditative practices. The Upanishads focus on understanding the nature of the self (*atman*), the ultimate reality (*Brahman*), and the relationship between the two. One of the key teachings of the Upanishads is that the individual soul (*atman*) is identical to the universal soul (*Brahman*), which is the source of all existence.

The Upanishads also introduced concepts such as *karma* (the law of moral causation), *samsara* (the cycle of birth, death, and rebirth), and *moksha* (liberation from the cycle of rebirth). These ideas would become central to Hindu philosophy and practice, shaping how Hindus understood their place in the universe and their spiritual goals.

The Upanishadic teachings emphasised personal introspection and spiritual knowledge over ritualism. This philosophical tradition laid the groundwork for later developments in Hindu thought, including the six classical schools of Hindu philosophy (*Shad Darshanas*), which include:

1. **Sankhya**: A dualistic philosophy distinguishing between matter (*Prakriti*) and consciousness (*Purusha*).
2. **Yoga**: A spiritual and physical practice that seeks to control the mind and senses, leading to liberation.
3. **Nyaya**: A school focused on logic and epistemology.
4. **Vaisheshika**: A system that explores the nature of reality through atomistic theory.
5. **Mimamsa**: A school that emphasises the importance of Vedic rituals and ethics.

6. **Vedanta**: A non-dualistic philosophy that teaches the unity of *Atman* and *Brahman*.

The Epics and Puranas: Shaping Hindu History and Practice

Alongside the Upanishads' philosophical developments, Hinduism evolved through its rich history, preserved in two of India's greatest epics: the Mahabharata, the *Ramayana*, and the *Puranas*.

- The Mahabharata, composed between the 4th century BCE and the 4th century CE, is an epic narrative about the Kurukshetra War and the moral dilemmas the characters involved face. Within the Mahabharata is the *Bhagavad Gita*, a text of immense spiritual significance, in which the god Krishna instructs the warrior Arjuna on duty, devotion, and the nature of reality. The *Bhagavad Gita* has become one of the most revered texts in Hinduism. She addresses key issues such as the path to liberation through devotion (*bhakti*), knowledge (*jnana*), and selfless action (*karma yoga*).

- Traditionally attributed to the sage Valmiki, the Ramayana tells the story of Prince Rama's quest to rescue his wife, Sita, from the demon king Ravana. The Ramayana explores themes of duty, righteousness, and the ideal relationship between individuals and society. Like the Mahabharata, the Ramayana has shaped Hindu values and ethical conduct.
- The Puranas, composed between the 3rd and 10th centuries CE, provide many legends, and genealogies of gods, sages, and kings. They introduce the

pantheon of Hindu deities—such as Vishnu, Shiva, and Devi—and their various incarnations and manifestations. The Puranas also emphasise devotional worship (*bhakti*), which became a major focus of Hindu practice in the medieval period.

Hindu Practices: Worship, Rituals, and the Pursuit of Moksha

Hinduism encompasses various religious practices, rituals, and forms of worship. These practices often vary depending on regional traditions, sects, and communities but share certain common elements. One of the defining features of Hinduism is its pluralistic nature, which allows for a diversity of paths to spiritual fulfilment.

- **Deity Worship (*Puja*)**: Hindus worship many deities, who are seen as manifestations of the one ultimate reality (*Brahman*). Major deities include Vishnu (the preserver), Shiva (the destroyer), and Devi (the goddess or divine feminine). Worship often involves offering flowers, food, and prayers at home altars or temples. Temples are central to Hindu religious life, serving as places of community gathering and spiritual devotion.

- **Meditation and Yoga**: Meditation is a key practice in Hinduism, aimed at calming the mind and realising the true nature of the self. *Yoga*, in its many forms, is a spiritual discipline that includes physical postures, breath control, and meditation, all designed to lead the practitioner toward self-realisation and liberation (*moksha*).
- **Rituals and Festivals**: Hindu rituals are diverse and often tied to key life events, such as birth,

marriage, and death. They are also closely associated with the changing seasons and the lunar calendar. Major Hindu festivals include the following.

- *Diwali*: The festival of lights, celebrating the victory of light over darkness.
- *Holi*: The festival of colours, celebrating the arrival of spring and the triumph of good over evil.
- *Navaratri*: A nine-night festival dedicated to the worship of the goddess Durga.
- *Maha Shivaratri*: A night dedicated to the worship of Lord Shiva.
- **Pursuit of Moksha**: Hindu life aims to achieve moksha, or liberation from the cycle of samsara (rebirth). This can be attained through various paths, including the following.

- ***Karma Yoga***: The path of selfless action, where one performs duties without attachment to the fruits of their labour.
- ***Bhakti Yoga***: The path of devotion, one surrenders to a personal deity and seeks divine grace.
- ***Jnana Yoga***: The path of knowledge, where one seeks to understand the nature of the self and its unity with Brahman.

Hindu Texts: A Wealth of Spiritual Wisdom

Hinduism's vast body of sacred texts can be attributed to its flexibility and ability to absorb and adapt to various cultural and philosophical influences. The primary texts of Hinduism are divided into two categories.

- **Shruti (That Which Is Heard)**: This includes the Vedas and the

Upanishads, considered divinely revealed. The Vedas are the oldest and most authoritative scriptures, while the Upanishads offer deep philosophical reflections on the nature of existence.

- **Smriti (That Which Is Remembered)**: This includes the epics (*Mahabharata* and *Ramayana*), the Puranas, and the *Dharma Shastras* (legal and ethical treatises). These texts guide righteous living and are the foundation of Hindu law and ethics.

Diversity in Hinduism: Schools, Sects, and Philosophies

Hinduism is not a monolithic tradition but a collection of diverse sects, schools of thought, and philosophical traditions. This diversity allows Hindus to practice their faith differently, depending on their inclinations, family traditions, and regional customs.

- **Vaishnavism**: The worship of Vishnu and his avatars, such as Krishna and Rama.
- **Shaivism**: Shiva's worship represents both destruction and regeneration.
- **Shaktism**: Worshipping *Shakti*, the divine feminine power or goddess. Followers of Shaktism revere the goddesses Durga, Kali, Lakshmi, and Saraswati, who are seen as manifestations of the supreme cosmic force. Shaktism emphasizes the importance of feminine energy in the cosmic balance.
- **Smartism**: A more philosophical and inclusive sect that reveres five deities—Vishnu, Shiva, Shakti, Ganesha, and Surya (the sun god)—as manifestations of the same divine reality, *Brahman*.

This sect allows for worshipping multiple gods but upholds the idea that all paths lead to the same ultimate truth.

Philosophical Pluralism in Hinduism

Hinduism's strength lies in its philosophical pluralism. Different schools of thought within Hinduism provide various ways of understanding the nature of reality, the self, and the divine. Individuals can pursue a path that resonates most with their beliefs and spiritual goals. While the schools differ in their interpretations, they all share karma, *dharma* (duty), and *moksha* (liberation) concepts.

- **Non-Dualism (Advaita Vedanta)**: One of the most influential schools of thought in Hinduism is *Advaita Vedanta*, which teaches that the individual self (*atman*) and the ultimate reality (*Brahman*) are the same.

According to this philosophy, the world of diversity and difference is an illusion (*Maya*), and human life aims to realise the underlying unity of all existence. This school was popularised by the philosopher Adi Shankaracharya in the 8th century CE.

- **Dualism (Dvaita)**: In contrast to Advaita Vedanta, the *Dvaita* (dualistic) school, championed by the philosopher Madhvacharya, posits that God (*Vishnu*) and the individual soul are eternally distinct. In Dvaita, God is a personal being with whom individuals have a loving relationship, and liberation is achieved through devotion to Him.
- **Qualified Non-Dualism (Vishishtadvaita)**: This school, founded by the philosopher Ramanuja, teaches that while *Atman* and *Brahman* are connected, they are not identical.

God is seen as both the creator and sustainer of the universe and the individual soul retains its distinctiveness even in union with God.

These schools of thought reflect the rich diversity within Hindu philosophy and the multiple paths for seeking truth and liberation.

Hinduism's Flexibility and Absorption of Cultural Influences

One of Hinduism's hallmarks is its remarkable ability to absorb and adapt to various cultural, philosophical, and religious influences throughout history. Over the centuries, Hinduism has evolved by incorporating elements from different traditions while maintaining its core spiritual teachings.

- **Influence of Buddhism and Jainism**: Buddhism and Jainism emerged as critiques of early Hinduism's ritualistic and caste-based practices in ancient India. While these religions introduced new ideas, such as non-violence (*ahimsa*) and renunciation, Hinduism absorbed many ethical teachings. By medieval India, Hinduism had re-emphasized devotional worship (*bhakti*) and meditation as key spiritual practices, drawing inspiration from Buddhist and Jain traditions.

- **Medieval Bhakti Movement**: The *Bhakti* movement flourished in medieval India and was a holy response to the rigidities of caste and ritualism. Saints like Ramanuja, Kabir, Tulsidas, and Mirabai popularised the worship of personal deities like Vishnu, Shiva, and the goddess. They taught that love and devotion to God were more important than caste distinctions or elaborate rituals. The Bhakti movement democratised religious practices, making them accessible to everyone regardless of caste or gender.

- **Islamic Influence**: During the medieval period, when Muslim dynasties ruled large parts of India, Hinduism interacted with Islam. Although the two religions remained distinct, Sufi mysticism and devotional practices influenced the Bhakti movement, and a cultural exchange enriched both traditions.
- **Modern Influences**: Hinduism has continued to evolve in the contemporary era, interacting with Western philosophical and scientific ideas. Reform movements like those led by Swami Vivekananda and Sri Aurobindo have emphasised social justice, non-violence, and spiritual universalism, presenting

Hinduism as a progressive and dynamic tradition.

Hinduism in the Modern World

Hinduism remains a major world religion, with over a billion followers, primarily in India and Nepal. Hindu communities can also be found across the globe, particularly in countries with large Indian diasporas, such as the United States, Canada, the United Kingdom, and South Africa.

Hinduism continues to evolve in the modern world while preserving its ancient traditions. Festivals, pilgrimages, and temple worship remain central to Hindu religious life, while philosophical inquiry, yoga, and meditation are increasingly popular within and outside Hinduism. Hindu ideas, particularly those related to non-violence, self-realisation, and the unity of all beings, have profoundly influenced global spiritual and philosophical thought.

Conclusion

The origins of the world's major religions provide invaluable insights into how humanity has sought to understand existence, morality, and the divine across different cultural and historical landscapes. Each religion— Buddhism, Judaism, Christianity, Islam, Sikhism, and Hinduism—emerged in response to specific social, political, and spiritual needs of their time. Yet, they all continue to shape the modern world profoundly. Their teachings, moral frameworks, and rituals have provided spiritual guidance and influenced the development of legal systems, human rights, and ethical governance in many parts of the world.

In the contemporary global order, these religions play a vital role in maintaining cultural identity and social cohesion while fostering interfaith dialogues to promote peace and understanding in an increasingly interconnected world. As globalisation brings diverse communities into closer contact, the teachings of these religions on compassion, justice, and coexistence remain highly relevant, offering paths to mitigate conflicts and build inclusive societies.

Moreover, these religious traditions' values of equality, social justice, and the pursuit of truth resonate with many modern movements for human rights, environmental sustainability, and social equity. From Buddhism's focus on ending suffering and promoting mindfulness to Islam's emphasis on social justice and Sikhism's advocacy for equality, these teachings offer practical wisdom for addressing some of the most pressing issues of the 21st century, such as inequality, climate change, and conflict resolution.

In essence, the continued relevance of these religions in the modern world order reflects their enduring ability to adapt and provide meaning to human life. They help billions of people navigate the complexities of existence while fostering hope for a just and harmonious world.

References

1. Armstrong, K. (1993). A History of God: The 4,000-Year Quest of Judaism, Christianity and Islam. New York: Ballantine Books.
2. Armstrong, K. (2000). Muhammad: A Biography of the Prophet.
3. Crossan, J. D. (1994). Jesus: A Revolutionary Biography. HarperSanFrancisco.
4. Doniger, W. (2009). The Hindus: An Alternative History. Penguin Books.
5. Ehrman, B. D. (2005). Misquoting Jesus: The Story Behind Who Changed the Bible and Why. HarperCollins.
6. Esposito, J. L. (2002). What Everyone Needs to Know About Islam.
7. Flood, G. (1996). An Introduction to Hinduism. Cambridge University Press.
8. Harvey, P. (2013). An Introduction to Buddhism: Teachings, History and Practices. Cambridge University Press.
9. Johnson, P. (1987). A History of the Jews. London: Weidenfeld & Nicolson.

10.   McLeod, W. H. (2005). The Sikhs: History, Religion, and Society. Oxford University Press.

11.   Singh, K. (1999). A History of the Sikhs: 1469–1839. Oxford University Press.

Comparing Hinduism, Buddhism, and Sikhism

Hinduism, Buddhism, and Sikhism are three prominent religions that have shaped the spiritual and cultural landscape of the Indian subcontinent. While distinct in their beliefs and practices, these religions share common historical roots and have influenced one another over centuries. This essay compares these three religions, focusing on their origins, key scriptures, philosophical underpinnings, and practices. The analysis will identify the commonalities and the divergences that characterise these faiths, offering a deeper understanding of their unique contributions to the spiritual traditions of the world.

Description of Hinduism, Buddhism, and Sikhism

Hinduism is one of the oldest religions in the world, with origins that trace back to the ancient Indus Valley Civilization. It has no founder but is a conglomeration of various beliefs, practices, and schools of thought that have evolved over millennia. Hinduism is primarily based on many scriptures, including the Vedas, Upanishads, Puranas, and the Bhagavad Gita. These texts guide various aspects of life, including philosophy, ethics, and spirituality. Important proponents of Hinduism include sages like Vyasa, who compiled the Vedas, and Adi Shankaracharya, who consolidated the doctrine of Advaita Vedanta.

Buddhism originated in the 6th century BCE with the teachings of Siddhartha Gautama, known as the Buddha, in northern India. Buddhism was born out of rejecting certain aspects of Hinduism, particularly the caste system and the rituals associated with Brahmanism. Buddhist teachings focus on the

Four Noble Truths and the Eightfold Path, which provide a framework for overcoming suffering and achieving enlightenment (Nirvana). The primary scriptures of Buddhism include the Tripitaka (Pali Canon), Mahayana Sutras, and Tibetan texts. Prominent figures in Buddhism include the Buddha himself and later teachers like Nagarjuna and Ashoka.

Sikhism was founded in the 15th century CE by Guru Nanak in the Punjab region of India. Sikhism arose during religious and social upheaval, incorporating Hindu and Islamic teachings while establishing a monotheistic faith. The primary scripture of Sikhism is the Guru Granth Sahib, a compilation of hymns and writings by Guru Nanak and the subsequent Sikh Gurus. Sikhism emphasises the belief in one formless, all-pervading God, Akal Purakh, and the importance of living a truthful, honest, and service-oriented life. The ten Sikh Gurus, including Guru Nanak and Guru Gobind Singh, are central figures in Sikhism.

Similarities

Hinduism, Buddhism, and Sikhism share similarities due to their cultural and philosophical heritage in the Indian subcontinent. One of the most significant similarities is their emphasis on Dharma, the ethical and moral principles that guide human behaviour. While Dharma in Hinduism is deeply rooted in the Vedic tradition, Buddhism and Sikhism also stress the importance of righteous living according to their respective teachings.

Buddhism and Sikhism originated as reform movements within the broader context of Hinduism. Buddhism emerged as a response to the rigidities of the caste system and the ceremonial practices of Brahmanism. At the same time, Sikhism sought to bridge the divide between Hinduism and Islam, emphasising a more egalitarian and inclusive approach to spirituality. Additionally, Buddhism and Sikhism follow a particular person or set of persons—Buddha in Buddhism and the ten Gurus in Sikhism.

Furthermore, both Hinduism and Sikhism believe in the existence of a single, formless Supreme Being. In Hinduism, this is referred to as Brahman, the ultimate reality that pervades the universe, while in Sikhism, it is Akal Purakh, the timeless and all-pervading God. Buddhism, however, diverges on this point, as it does not posit the existence of a creator god or supreme being.

Differences

Despite their similarities, Hinduism, Buddhism, and Sikhism differ significantly in their doctrines, practices, and worldviews. One of the primary differences lies in their views on divinity. Hinduism is a polytheistic religion with a belief in a supreme Brahman and a pantheon of deities representing various aspects of life and nature. In contrast, Sikhism is strictly monotheistic, emphasising the worship of one God without any form or image. On the other hand, Buddhism does not focus on the worship of gods but rather on pursuing enlightenment through self-discipline and meditation.

The concept of scripture also differs among these religions. Hinduism holds the Vedas, Upanishads, Puranas, and the Bhagavad Gita as sacred and canonical texts. In contrast, Sikhism regards the Guru Granth Sahib as the final and eternal Guru, containing the teachings of the Sikh Gurus and other saints. However, Buddhism has a more diverse collection of scriptures, including the Pali Canon and Mahayana Sutras, with no fixed canon recognised by all Buddhist schools.

Another key difference is the role of rituals and practices. Hinduism is rich in traditions, ceremonies, and a variety of paths (margas) for spiritual advancement, including Bhakti (devotion), Karma (action), and Jnana (knowledge). Sikhism, however, rejects many of the ritualistic practices of Hinduism and Islam, focusing instead on simple worship and the recitation of God's name (Naam Japna). Buddhism strongly emphasises meditation, ethical conduct, and the monastic life to achieve Nirvana.

The concept of ego and self-realisation is another area of divergence. Hinduism believes in the idea of Maya, the illusionary world that binds individuals to the cycle of birth and death, and the need to transcend the ego (Ahamkara) to realise the self. Sikhism shares a similar belief, referring to the ego as Haumai, which hinders a person's connection with God. Buddhism, however, teaches the doctrine of Anatta (non-self), which denies the existence of a permanent self or soul and emphasises the impermanent nature of all things.

Conclusion

Hinduism, Buddhism, and Sikhism, while sharing a common cultural and historical background, have evolved into distinct religions with unique philosophies and practices. As the oldest of the three, Hinduism provided the philosophical and spiritual foundation from which Buddhism and Sikhism emerged. However, each religion has charted its path, addressing the spiritual needs of its followers in different ways. Hinduism's diversity, Buddhism's focus on enlightenment, and Sikhism's emphasis on monotheism and social justice reflect the rich and varied spiritual landscape of the Indian subcontinent. Understanding these similarities and differences provides valuable insights into the religious and cultural dynamics that continue to shape the region and the world.

References

1. Flood, Gavin. An Introduction to Hinduism. Cambridge University Press, 1996.
2. Keown, Damien. Buddhism: A Very Short Introduction. Oxford University Press, 2013.
3. McLeod, W. H. Sikhism: A Very Short Introduction. Oxford University Press, 2010.

4. Radhakrishnan, S. Indian Philosophy: Volume 1. Oxford University Press, 2008.
5. Singh, Khushwant. The History of Sikhs: Volume 1: 1469-1839. Oxford University Press, 2004.

The Number 13: A Symbol of Superstition, Tradition, and Spiritual Significance

The number 13 is one of history's most discussed and debated numbers. It has been perceived as a symbol of bad luck, spiritual transition, and even divine significance in various cultures and religious traditions. This article explores the historical connotations of the number 13 in the Western world, its importance in Hinduism, and its roles in other spiritual traditions, including Buddhism, Jainism, Sikhism, and Islam.

The Unlucky Number 13 in the Western World

In Western cultures, the number 13 is often regarded as unlucky, a belief known as "triskaidekaphobia." This superstition is so widespread that many buildings skip the 13th floor, labelling it as the 14th instead. The origins of this belief are complex and multifaceted, rooted in history, mythology, and religion.

One prominent theory connects the fear of 13 to the Last Supper in Christianity, where 13 individuals (Jesus and his 12 apostles) were present. Judas Iscariot, who betrayed Jesus, is often considered the 13th guest, which added to the number's association with treachery and misfortune.

Another historical perspective points to Norse mythology, where Loki, the trickster god, crashed a dinner party of 12 gods, making him the 13th guest. His arrival led to the death of the beloved god Balder, reinforcing the idea that 13 brings misfortune.

The number 13 is also linked with various dark events in history. For example, the mass arrest and persecution of the Knights Templar began on Friday, October 13th, 1307, under the orders of King Philip IV of France. This event further solidified the number's negative connotations in Western consciousness.

The Spiritual Significance of 13 in Hinduism

In Hindu tradition, the number 13 holds a deep spiritual significance, particularly concerning death and mourning. After a person's death, Hindus believe that the soul lingers around the house for 13 days. During this period, the family observes a mourning phase, refraining from various daily activities as a sign of respect and remembrance.

On the 13th day, a ritual known as the "Shraddha" or "Terahvin" is performed. This ritual is believed to help the soul transition from the earthly realm to the afterlife, allowing it to move towards the holy abode. The number 13, in this context, symbolises the completion of the mourning period and the beginning of the soul's spiritual journey.

This practice is not just limited to Hinduism. Similar rituals are observed in Buddhism, Jainism, and Sikhism, religions that share common roots with Hinduism. For instance, Buddhists also observe rituals after death, although the specifics may vary based on cultural practices. Jainism and Sikhism, which emphasise the cycle of birth and rebirth, also incorporate rituals to aid the soul's journey after death, often marking important days in mourning.

The Role of 13 in Islam

In contrast to the Western and Hindu interpretations, the number 13 does not hold the same superstitious or spiritual significance in Islam. However, it is only partially absent from Islamic thought. The number 13 can be found in some numerological interpretations within Islamic mysticism, though it is not a widely emphasised number.

One of the few mentions is in certain esoteric interpretations of the Quran, where numbers are seen as having deeper, mystical meanings. Some scholars have pointed out that there are 13 letters in the "Bismillah" (the opening phrase of the Quran), but this is not a universally recognised significance within Islam. Generally, Islam does not attribute religious importance or superstition to the number 13.

Conclusion

13 is a fascinating example of how numbers can carry different meanings across cultures and religions. It is predominantly seen as an unlucky number in the Western world, a belief rooted in historical, religious, and mythological events. In Hinduism, the number 13 has a profound spiritual significance, marking the end of the mourning period and the beginning of the soul's journey in the afterlife. While Buddhism, Jainism, and Sikhism share similar practices with Hinduism, Islam does not emphasise the number 13 in any religious context.

The number 13 reminds us of how cultures and religions interpret the world around them, often imbuing even the simplest numbers with rich, complex meanings.

References

1. "Why Is 13 Considered Unlucky?" History.com, accessed August 9, 2024. (https://www.history.com/news/why-is-13-considered-unlucky)
2. "Triskaidekaphobia: Fear of the Number 13 and Its Origins." Live Science, accessed August 9, 2024. (https://www.livescience.com/why-13-unlucky.html)
3. "The Number 13: Superstitions and Symbolism." ThoughtCo., accessed August 9, 2024. (https://www.thoughtco.com/the-number-13-superstitions-and-symbolism-3890146)
4. "Friday the 13th and the Knights Templar." National Geographic, accessed August 9, 2024.

(https://www.nationalgeographic.com/history/article/friday-the-13th-knights-templar-history)

5. "The Significance of the Number 13 in Hinduism." Hinduism Today, accessed August 9, 2024. (https://www.hinduismtoday.com/)

6. "Death and Mourning in Hinduism, Buddhism, and Jainism." Oxford Research Encyclopedia of Religion accessed August 9, 2024. (https://oxfordre.com/religion/view/10.1093/acrefore/9780199340378.001.0001/acrefore-9780199340378-e-28)

7. "Sikh Rituals and Death Ceremonies." SikhNet, accessed August 9, 2024. (https://www.sikhnet.com/pages/sikh-rituals-and-death-ceremonies)

8. "Islamic Numerology and the Significance of Numbers." The Muslim Vibe, accessed August 9, 2024. (https://themuslimvibe.com/faith-islam/islamic-numerology-and-the-significance-of-numbers)

Why Do We Have Wars?

Wars have plagued human history for millennia, raising the inevitable question: why do we have wars? At the heart of the answer may lie in the very design of the universe, a balance between good and bad, light and darkness, peace and conflict. In this article, I will explore the interplay of divine design, human perception, and historical struggles to shed light on the roots of war.

Creation's Duality: The Good and the Bad

When God created the universe, He instilled within it both the good and the bad, a duality essential for maintaining balance. This design is visible everywhere in nature—day and night, life and death, joy and sorrow. This idea of inherent opposition isn't just a theological or philosophical notion; it can also be found in science, such as the concept of matter and antimatter or the opposing forces of attraction and repulsion in physics. Wars, in this sense, are manifestations of this broader cosmic duality—a struggle between competing forces, whether ideologies, resources, or survival.

A classic example is the Cold War, a prolonged ideological and geopolitical battle between the capitalist West, led by the United States, and the communist East, led by the Soviet Union. While not always erupting into direct warfare, the constant tension reflected the larger struggle between perceived good (freedom, democracy) and bad (authoritarianism, oppression). The existence of these opposing forces maintained a delicate balance, even when it seemed like the world teetered on the brink of destruction.

The Struggle Between Good and Bad

History shows that the struggle between good and bad is a constant in human civilisation, driven by the universal need to seek balance.

However, what is defined as good or bad often depends on who emerges victorious. As they say, the winners write history, and thus, they are usually portrayed as the righteous force, while the losers are depicted as the villains. History is more complex.

Take, for example, the American Revolutionary War. From the colonists' perspective, the war was a righteous battle for freedom from tyranny. However, from the British side, it could be seen as a rebellion against a lawful authority. Similarly, in World War II, the Allies are remembered as the champions of justice, defeating the evil axis of fascism and dictatorship. Yet even within the narrative of the "good guys," there are darker aspects, such as the use of atomic bombs on Hiroshima and Nagasaki, acts still debated for their moral consequences. History's moral labels of good and bad often depend on who tells the story.

This brings us to a larger question: is God always with the victors, as history often suggests? If the winners are viewed as good and the losers as bad, it reinforces the belief that God must favour the victorious side. Yet, history also contains examples of unjust wars and aggressions where the victors may have committed atrocities, such as the colonisation of the Americas, where indigenous populations were decimated in the name of expansion and conquest. In these cases, the winners may not necessarily be on the side of good, complicating the notion of divine favour.

Divine Intervention to Restore Balance

When the balance between good and bad tips too far in one direction, many traditions believe that God intervenes to restore equilibrium. This divine intervention often manifests through a saviour or a transformative event that realigns the moral or spiritual order of the world. In the Bhagavad Gita, Krishna explains that whenever righteousness falters, and evil rises,

He incarnates to protect the good and destroy the wicked, restoring cosmic order.

In Christian tradition, there is the story of Noah's Ark. When humanity's wickedness became overwhelming, God intervened by sending a great flood to cleanse the earth. The few righteous people, led by Noah, were spared, allowing humanity to start anew on a more virtuous path. Similarly, the story of Moses leading the Israelites out of Egypt can be seen as God's intervention to restore justice to His chosen people, oppressed by the Pharaoh's tyranny.

Even in modern history, wars often serve as agents of change, shifting power dynamics, addressing injustices, or realigning geopolitical boundaries. The American Civil War, for example, can be seen as a necessary but brutal intervention to abolish slavery and move the nation towards greater equality and justice. While the cost was tremendous, the ultimate restoration of balance—freedom for millions of enslaved people—was a moral necessity.

Conclusion

Wars seem like an inherent contradiction to the ideal of a peaceful, ordered universe. Still, they are, in a sense, inevitable outcomes of the world's fundamental design of duality—good versus bad. This struggle has shaped human history, with victors often dictating how we perceive these forces. However, even as wars disrupt, they may restore balance when the scales have tipped too far toward chaos or injustice.

Ultimately, wars remind us of the ongoing tension between opposing forces in the universe and the belief that divine intervention—whether through human actions or extraordinary events—restores balance when the world falls out of harmony. The lesson may not be that wars are desirable but that conflict is an unfortunate but inevitable means of maintaining equilibrium in a universe defined by duality.

Hard Work Never Kills

The tragic incident involving the death of Anna, an Ernst and Young (EY) employee in India, has sparked discussions about the pressures of modern work environments. While the circumstances surrounding her death are deeply saddening, I firmly believe that hard work never kills. History provides numerous examples of individuals who dedicated their lives to great tasks without succumbing to the weight of their efforts.

Hard Work in the Indian Context

There are countless stories in India of people who have taken on seemingly impossible tasks, surviving and thriving through sheer perseverance. Take Dashrath Manjhi, known as the "Mountain Man," who spent over 22 years single-handedly carving a path through a mountain to connect his village to medical care. His work was physically exhausting, far more taxing than the white-collar work done in air-conditioned offices today, yet he remained determined and alive throughout.

Similarly, Jadav Payeng, known as the "Forest Man of India," transformed barren land into a forest by planting trees for over 50 years. His task was not only physically demanding but required immense dedication and patience. He, too, did not perish from his work's intensity but left a legacy.

While the pressure can feel overwhelming in white-collar jobs, we can access resources like air conditioning, nutritious food, water, and breaks that physically taxing labourers lack. This distinction makes it clear that hard work is not the direct cause of death, particularly in an office setting. The human body is capable of extraordinary endurance when balanced with appropriate self-care.

Insights from the Ramayan and Mahabharat

The Indian epics Ramayan and Mahabharat also provide valuable insights into hard work, duty, and perseverance. In the Ramayan, Lord Ram spends 14 years in exile, during which he faces immense hardships, including the physical strain of living in forests and battling demons. Yet, his dedication to dharma (righteousness) and his commitment to his mission always continue. Lord Ram's life shows us that hard work, no matter how challenging, is a pathway to growth and purpose, not death.

In the Mahabharat, Arjun is a shining example of a warrior who endures incredible mental and physical strain to fulfil his duty. During the Kurukshetra war, Arjun's challenges are both emotional and physical, yet his adherence to his purpose bolsters his resilience. Krishna's guidance to Arjun in the Shrimad Bhagavad Gita reinforces the idea that one should work without attachment to the results, focusing on performing one's duty rather than worrying about the outcomes.

Krishna's words—Karmanye Vadhikaraste, Ma Phaleshu Kadachana—mean that we are entitled to work but not to the fruits of our labour. This profound message reminds us that life's purpose lies in continuous effort, not in the fear of consequences or the illusion that hard work is fatal.

Ayurvedic Perspective on Individual Constitution and Endurance

In the ancient Indian system of medicine, Ayurved, it is believed that every individual is born with a unique constitution known as Prakriti. This constitution, determined at birth, shapes one's physical, mental, and emotional characteristics, including endurance levels and responses to stress. According to Ayurvedic principles, Prakriti is governed by three primary doshas: Vata, Pitta, and Kapha, and the combination of these doshas determines the individual's strengths, weaknesses, and natural abilities.

An individual's constitution influences their physical resilience, mental fortitude, and capacity for hard work. Ayurvedic experts can assess a person's Prakriti to identify health and endurance imbalances. Through personalised dietary changes, lifestyle modifications, herbal treatments, and yoga practices, Ayurveda helps individuals maintain balance, ensuring their body and mind are better equipped to handle stress and hard work.

Ayurved thus recognises that what may be overwhelming for one person might be manageable for another, based on their inherent constitution. This understanding emphasises the importance of individualised approaches to well-being and endurance, suggesting that with proper adjustments, anyone can optimise their capacity for hard work and resilience.

Hard Work and the Uncertainty of Life

No one can predict when or how one will die. Life is unpredictable, and death is an inevitable end for us all. Instead of fearing hard work or believing it to cause death, we should embrace our responsibilities with dedication and purpose. The tragedy of Anna's death is a painful reminder of life's fragility, but it should not deter us from working hard and striving to make a difference. After all, those who truly leave a mark on this world persevere through challenges and contribute something meaningful.

While the pressures of modern life and work can be significant, they are not the reason for death. It is not the hard work but often the imbalance, stress, or underlying health issues that may contribute to such outcomes. Maintaining a balance between physical and mental well-being and hard work is crucial. The stories of people who have worked tirelessly for decades show us that it is possible to take on enormous tasks without succumbing to them.

Consider the case of Srinivasa Ramanujan, one of India's greatest mathematical minds. Despite enduring immense hardship, illness, and working under strenuous conditions in India and England, Ramanujan's passion for mathematics kept him going. He worked relentlessly, making groundbreaking contributions to number theory and infinite series despite being largely self-taught. Although his life was tragically cut short due to health reasons, his hard work and dedication to his field left an indelible mark on mathematics. His premature death was not due to the work itself but to underlying health issues, proving that it's the imbalance or circumstances rather than the work that may cause harm.

Similarly, the prolific American inventor Thomas Alva Edison is another example of tireless dedication. Edison worked for countless hours, famously stating, "Genius is 1% inspiration and 99% perspiration." He held over a thousand patents and was known for his rigorous work ethic, often experimenting through the night. Yet, he maintained his passion and enthusiasm throughout his life, showing that hard work drives innovation and is not a cause for health concerns.

Both figures exemplify that hard work, with passion and a balanced approach, can lead to remarkable achievements without detrimentally damaging one's life or well-being. Their legacies testify that purposeful work brings fulfilment and long-lasting societal contributions.

Conclusion

The idea that hard work can kill is a misconception. Throughout history and modern times, we find examples of individuals who have dedicated their lives to immense tasks, pushing their physical and mental boundaries. Their hard work did not lead to their demise but rather to a legacy. We must recognise that while life is fleeting, the best way to live is through purposeful work, aiming to impact the world positively. When balanced with care and mindfulness, hard work does not kill—it builds, creates, and leaves a legacy that transcends life.

Do Not Procrastinate

Procrastination is a habit that prevents many from reaching their full potential. By delaying tasks, we reduce our efficiency and increase stress and anxiety. The key to overcoming procrastination lies in acting on thoughts as they arise and applying principles of agility to personal life. Here, I will walk through actionable steps with real-life examples of how to stop procrastination and live in the present.

When a Thought Comes to Mind, Note It Down and Mark the Time

Every task or idea begins with a simple thought. Successful individuals know the power of recording these thoughts before they slip away. Consider Richard Branson, the founder of the Virgin Group. Branson is known for always carrying a notebook, capturing every idea, no matter how trivial. By noting down thoughts immediately, he ensures that no potential innovation or solution is lost to procrastination. His practice has allowed him to juggle multiple businesses successfully.

This practice has become even easier with smartphones offering note-taking apps and voice memo features in today's modern world. Unlike Richard Branson's reliance on a physical notebook, we now have the convenience of recording thoughts instantly with just a few taps. Whether in a meeting, on the move, or simply away from your desk, capturing ideas quickly ensures that none are forgotten, enabling you to stay organised and focused on immediate action.

Start Work on the Thought as Quickly as Possible

Taking quick action on ideas is crucial. Once a thought is noted, the next step is to start work on it immediately. Elon Musk, CEO of Tesla and SpaceX, is famous for his aggressive timelines. When he sets a goal, he starts working toward it without delay. For instance, when Musk announced the development of Tesla's Gigafactory, many thought of his ambitious timeline. However, by avoiding procrastination and jumping straight into action, Musk built the factory ahead of schedule. This proactive mindset prevents thoughts from stagnating and turns ideas into reality.

We can draw from the wisdom of Kabir, the 15th-century mystic poet, who emphasised the importance of immediate action and the fleeting nature of time. One of Kabir's most famous sayings is:

"Kal kare so aaj kar, aaj kare so ab"

"Pal mein parlay hoyegi, bahuri karega kab?"

This translates to "What you plan to do tomorrow, do today, and what you plan to do today, do it right now. Catastrophe may strike in a moment—how will you finish it then?"

Kabir's words strongly resonate with the philosophy of acting swiftly on thoughts and ideas. Just as Elon Musk believes in working toward goals without delay, Kabir reminds us that postponing action can result in lost opportunities. Time waits for no one, and swift action ensures that tasks are completed before unforeseen circumstances derail progress. This lesson teaches us to avoid procrastination and turn ideas into reality without hesitation. Kabir's timeless wisdom aligns with the proactive mindset that moves individuals like Musk to success.

Note the Time When the Thought Was Accomplished

Tracking the time to execute a task is an excellent way to monitor progress. For example, the iconic comedian Jerry Seinfeld uses a method he calls "Don't break the chain." He marks a calendar every time he writes new jokes. Seinfeld stayed motivated and disciplined by keeping track of his accomplishments, which ultimately contributed to his successful career. Tracking completion times builds accountability and ensures steady momentum.

In modern times, tracking accomplishments has become incredibly simple with apps like Reminder on Apple Mac and other similar tools. These apps allow users to set tasks, mark their completion, and even track the time taken to complete them. You can stay accountable and maintain steady progress using digital reminders and task trackers, just like Jerry Seinfeld's "Don't break the chain" method. Such tools help build discipline and ensure every task is completed on time, reducing procrastination.

Celebrate Every Accomplishment, However Small

Celebrating your accomplishments, no matter how small, is key to staying motivated. With the advent of social media, sharing your progress has become very easy. Platforms like Instagram, Twitter, or LinkedIn allow you to inform your friends and peers about your achievements, gaining encouragement and recognition. Personal gratification is essential in maintaining motivation; celebrating these moments gives you a sense of fulfilment. Whether you finish a small task or hit a major milestone, acknowledging your efforts can boost your confidence and drive you toward your next goal.

Gradually Reduce the Time Between the Arrival of Thoughts and Their Accomplishment

The goal is to progressively reduce the time between an idea's occurrence and execution. Steve Jobs was known for pushing his team to achieve faster innovation cycles during his tenure at Apple. Whether it was the first iPhone's development or the MacBook's evolution, Jobs constantly emphasised reducing the time between conception and execution. This relentless focus on swift execution helped Apple outpace competitors in an industry driven by rapid technological change. By aiming to minimise delays, we, too, can maximise productivity and stay ahead.

Make Decisions Quickly

Quick decision-making is another vital skill to prevent procrastination. While it's important to weigh options, delaying decisions can lead to lost opportunities. Rusy Modi, former chairman of Tata Steel, had a mechanism for rapid decision-making: "I make my decisions quickly. I may make mistakes. However, out of 100, more than 95 are correct decisions." Modi's approach emphasises the importance of action over perfection. He understood that waiting too long to make decisions often results in missed chances and stagnation. Like Modi, we must trust our instincts, accept that occasional mistakes are part of the process, and move forward quickly. Over time, this practice sharpens our judgment and reduces procrastination, ensuring tasks are completed efficiently.

Lord Krishna emphasises the importance of action without attachment to results in the Bhagavad Gita.

"Karmanye Vadhikaraste, Ma Phaleshu Kadachana" (Chapter 2, Verse 47), meaning "You have a right to perform your duty, but not to the fruits of your actions."

This teaching aligns perfectly with the message of avoiding procrastination. Instead of waiting for the perfect moment or ideal conditions, Krishna advises us to focus on doing our work promptly without worrying about the outcomes. By taking swift, deliberate action and concentrating on the process rather than the result, we overcome procrastination and cultivate a mindset that leads to inner peace and efficiency. This aligns well with modern productivity practices—acting quickly, learning from mistakes, and not letting fear of results delay us.

This Is the Way to Live in the Present

Reducing the gap between thought and action brings us closer to living in the present. Tim Ferriss, author of "*The 4-Hour Workweek*," advocates for reducing distractions and taking immediate action on important tasks to avoid mental clutter. Procrastination creates a backlog of unfinished tasks, pulling us away from the present moment and increasing stress. When we act swiftly, we free ourselves from the burden of future tasks, allowing us to focus fully on the present.

This Is an Agile Implementation in One's Personal Life

In the tech industry, agile methodologies emphasise flexibility and quick iteration. The same principles can be applied to personal life. When you shorten the cycle between thought and execution, you implement an agile mindset, constantly improving your process. For example, Jeff Bezos, founder of Amazon, implemented "two-pizza teams," small, agile teams that could react and execute quickly, reducing bottlenecks in decision-making. This agile philosophy has propelled Amazon's growth. By adopting this approach in your personal life, you can accomplish tasks with greater efficiency and adaptability.

Conclusion

Procrastination can hold us back from achieving our true potential. However, this can be overcome through quick, deliberate actions. Real-life examples like Richard Branson, Elon Musk, and Steve Jobs show how acting swiftly on ideas leads to success. Additionally, celebrating small accomplishments and making rapid decisions—using modern tools like apps and social media—helps maintain motivation and momentum. By embracing these agile principles, we can shorten the gap between thought and action, living fully in the present and boosting productivity, ultimately leading to personal fulfilment and long-lasting success.

The democratisation of Education in India: A Leap Forward with Room for Growth

In recent years, India has witnessed a significant shift in the accessibility of higher education, propelled by the digital revolution and the willingness of premier institutions to adapt and expand their reach. The hallowed halls of the Indian Institutes of Technology (IITs), Indian Institutes of Management (IIMs), Indian Institute of Science (IISc), and others have long been the preserve of the academically elite, accessible only to those who could surmount their rigorous entrance examinations. This exclusivity, while maintaining academic excellence, limited the broader societal impact these institutions could achieve.

The Online Education Wave

The landscape began to transform with the introduction of online programs by these esteemed institutions. Offering a range of short-term and long-term courses, these initiatives have opened new avenues for a larger demographic to benefit from high-quality education. Professionals seeking to upskill, students aiming to broaden their academic horizons, and lifelong learners keen on exploring new domains have found these programs to be a gateway to India's premier institutions' rich educational heritage and advanced learning methodologies.

Economic Barriers to Access

However, this democratisation is not without its challenges. The cost of these online programs often pegged at a premium, poses a significant barrier to a large population segment. While the digital format overcomes geographical constraints, economic barriers still must be overcome for brilliant students from economically weaker sections. This discrepancy raises questions about the inclusivity of these initiatives and whether true democratisation of education can be achieved without addressing the financial constraints a substantial portion of the potential student population faces.

Impact on Innovation

The expansion of access to premier institutions has not only democratised education but also democratised opportunity. Students from diverse backgrounds now have the chance to engage with cutting-edge research, collaborate on projects, and utilise state-of-the-art facilities such as labs and data sets. This confluence of varied perspectives is a potent catalyst for innovation. However, the accurate measure of success lies in the tangible outcomes of these educational endeavours. The critical question remains: How many of these students will leverage their newly acquired knowledge and resources to create innovations that address real-world challenges?

The Role of CxOs and Policymakers

As leaders in the corporate and public sectors, CxOs and ministers play a pivotal role in shaping the future of education in India. There is a growing need for public-private partnerships to address the financial barriers to education. Corporations can collaborate with educational institutions to sponsor scholarships, fund research projects, and create student internships and job opportunities. Similarly, government policies can incentivise businesses to invest in education and research, thereby broadening the impact of these premier institutions.

Furthermore, integrating online education with mainstream academic curricula can enhance its credibility and value in the job market. Encouraging innovation through competitions, incubation centres, and startup funding can turn academic projects into viable commercial ventures, closing the loop from education to entrepreneurship.

Conclusion: A Vision for Inclusive Education

The initiatives by India's premier institutions to offer online programs mark a significant step towards democratising education. However, concerted efforts from all stakeholders are essential for the vision of genuinely inclusive education to be realised. Bridging economic disparities, fostering an ecosystem that encourages innovation, and creating synergies between education and industry are crucial to unlocking the full potential of India's academic prowess.

As we navigate this transformation, we must remember that democratising education aims to broaden access and empower individuals to contribute meaningfully to society. By nurturing a generation of innovators, thinkers, and leaders, India can harness the collective intellectual capital of its populace to drive sustainable growth and development. The journey towards democratisation is ongoing, and with collaborative effort, the dream of accessible, high-quality education for all can become a reality.

Embracing Data Analytics Across Organisational Levels: Beyond the C-Suite

In the era of data dominance, data analytics has transcended its traditional boundaries, becoming an invaluable asset across sectors and organisational levels. This article explores the often-underestimated applications of data analytics, advocating for a more comprehensive and integrated organisational approach that can unlock new efficiencies, enhance decision-making, and pave the way for innovative solutions to traditional problems.

Revolutionising Resource Optimisation

In the dynamic world of investment banking, routine batch processes play a crucial role in daily operations. These essential yet often overlooked processes are the linchpins of the banking sector, ensuring that transactions are processed and reconciled efficiently. However, despite their importance, these batch processes frequently fall outside the purview of C-level executives regarding optimisation initiatives. This oversight can lead to significant resource consumption and operational inefficiencies, resulting in delays that can impede the overall functioning of the bank.

The key to revolutionising these processes lies in the strategic application of data analytics, mainly through machine learning and operations research. By systematically collecting and analysing data related to batch process operations, banks can identify patterns and inefficiencies that might not be apparent at first glance. This data-driven approach allows for developing models that can predict the optimal allocation of resources—be it computational power or human expertise—to ensure that batch processes are completed as efficiently and cost-effectively as possible.

Such an approach streamlines operations, making them more agile and responsive, and leads to significant cost reductions. The efficiency gains from optimising batch processes can free up valuable resources that can be redirected towards more strategic areas of the bank's operations, fostering innovation and competitive advantage.

Transforming IT Development and Maintenance

In the fast-paced realm of IT development, pursuing technological innovation often overshadows the need for optimisation within internal processes. Bug fixing, a routine yet crucial task in software development, exemplifies an area ripe for optimisation but frequently overlooked. This oversight can lead to prolonged development cycles and delayed product deliveries, impacting the organisation's ability to capitalise on new market opportunities.

Drawing inspiration from an unlikely source—the retail industry's Market Basket analysis—offers a novel approach to enhancing the bug-fixing process. Market Basket analysis, widely used in retail to understand customer purchase patterns, can be ingeniously applied to IT development to identify correlations among software bugs. Just as retailers analyse transaction data to predict product combinations likely to be purchased, IT departments can analyse historical bug data to identify patterns or groups of bugs that frequently occur together.

This predictive approach to bug fixing can significantly streamline the development process. By understanding bug correlations, developers can anticipate and address related issues in tandem, reducing the iterative cycles of debugging and testing. This not only accelerates the development process but also enhances the overall quality of the software product.

Moreover, using data analytics to optimise bug fixing can open new avenues for business growth. Faster system delivery means quicker time-to-market for new software products, providing a competitive edge in today's rapidly evolving technological landscape. Additionally, the resources saved through more efficient bug fixing can be reallocated to other strategic areas, further driving innovation and growth.

Conclusion

The transformation brought about by leveraging data analytics for resource optimisation in batch processes exemplifies the broader potential of data analytics across organisational levels. It highlights the need for managers and executives to look beyond conventional areas for optimisation and consider the untapped opportunities that data analytics presents to enhance operational efficiency and reduce costs. In doing so, organisations can ensure they are fully harnessing the power of their data to drive continuous improvement and sustainable growth.

The transformative potential of applying data analytics to IT development and maintenance underscores the broader theme that data analytics should not be confined to high-level strategic decisions but integrated across all levels of an organisation. By embracing data-driven optimisation strategies, IT departments—and organisations as a whole—can unlock new efficiencies, enhance product quality, and expedite innovation, ensuring sustained competitiveness in the digital age.

The untapped potential of data analytics is a goldmine for organisations ready to embrace a more integrated approach. By extending data analytics beyond the executive suite to all levels of management, organisations can unlock new efficiencies, enhance decision-making, and pave the way for innovative solutions to traditional problems. In a world increasingly driven by data, successful organisations will not just view data analytics as a tool for the C-suite but as an integral part of their operational and strategic fabric.

Focus on the Strengths

Every individual has a reservoir of unique strengths and talents, often waiting to be discovered and nurtured. When identified and leveraged, these strengths can lead to remarkable personal and collective growth. Understanding and focusing on these inherent abilities enhances individual well-being and significantly improves organisations and society. This idea is not new; ancient Indian texts like the Purans have long advocated recognising and nurturing one's innate strengths.

Uncovering Individual Strengths

Every person possesses a set of strengths that distinguish them from others. These might be cognitive abilities, interpersonal skills, creative talents, or technical expertise. The key to unlocking potential lies in recognising and harnessing these strengths. When individuals are encouraged to use their strengths, they tend to perform better, feel more satisfied, and exhibit higher levels of engagement and productivity.

The Vishnu Puran states, "Each being is a pillar of strength; acknowledging and nurturing one's strength brings forth divine capabilities." This ancient wisdom emphasises that recognising individual strengths leads to manifesting one's highest potential and aligning personal growth with divine purpose.

Maximising Potential Through Strengths

Focusing on what individuals do best can help us extract their maximum potential. This approach drives personal success and fosters a sense of accomplishment and self-worth. Acknowledging people's strengths enhances their confidence and motivates them to continue excelling. This positive reinforcement creates a virtuous cycle where individuals feel valued and inspired to contribute more effectively.

This principle can transform ordinary teams into super teams in an organisational context. By aligning tasks and responsibilities with team members' strengths, organisations can significantly boost performance and innovation. For instance, a team member with excellent analytical skills might thrive in a data-intensive role, while another with exceptional communication abilities could excel in client-facing positions. Such strategic alignment optimises output and fosters a collaborative and dynamic work environment.

The Bhagavata Puran teaches, "In unity lies strength; in division, weakness." This highlights the importance of focusing on a group's collective strengths to achieve unparalleled success and harmony.

Creating Super Teams in Organisations

Organisations that emphasise their employees' strengths often see remarkable efficiency and morale improvements. When team members are assigned roles that match their strengths, they are more likely to feel competent and motivated. This enhances individual job satisfaction and promotes a culture of mutual respect and collaboration. Teams that operate in this manner can tackle challenges more effectively, innovate more freely, and achieve their goals more efficiently.

The Mahabharata also echoes this sentiment: "A team united in purpose, harnessing each member's strength, shall overcome the greatest of challenges." By focusing on strengths, organisations can build resilient and innovative teams capable of achieving extraordinary results.

Applying the Principle in Social Life

The focus on strengths is equally applicable in social settings. Recognising and appreciating each other's strengths can lead to more harmonious and supportive relationships in families, communities, or friendships. In families, for example, understanding each member's unique talents can help distribute responsibilities so everyone feels valued and contributes effectively. In communities, leveraging members' diverse skills can lead to collective success and cohesion.

The Garuda Puran states, "In recognising the divine in others, we uplift our spirit." By appreciating and nurturing the strengths of those around us, we create a supportive and elevated community.

The Detrimental Impact of Focusing on Weaknesses

Conversely, an emphasis on weaknesses can have detrimental effects. When individuals are constantly reminded of their shortcomings, it erodes their self-esteem and confidence. This negative focus can lead to decreased motivation and engagement, ultimately hampering personal and professional growth. In organisations, a culture highlighting weaknesses over strengths can result in a disengaged workforce, high turnover rates, and a stifled innovation climate.

Similarly, in social contexts, focusing on weaknesses can strain relationships and create an environment of negativity and criticism. It can lead to feelings of inadequacy and resentment, undermining the sense of community and support essential for collective well-being.

The Matsya Puran warns, "To dwell on one's faults is to invite despair; to nurture strengths is to embrace divinity." This ancient wisdom underscores the destructive nature of focusing on weaknesses and the importance of fostering strengths.

Building a Strength-Based Culture

Several steps can be taken to build a strength-based culture in organisations and society. Firstly, it is essential to implement systems and practices that identify and celebrate individual strengths. This could involve regular feedback sessions, strength assessments, and opportunities for individuals to showcase their talents.

Secondly, it is crucial to foster an environment that encourages continuous learning and development. Organisations and communities can ensure sustained growth and improvement by providing resources and support for individuals to develop their strengths further.

Lastly, promoting a mindset shift towards recognising and valuing strengths over weaknesses can lead to a more positive and productive culture. This involves training leaders, managers, and community heads to focus on strengths-based development and creating platforms for sharing success stories and best practices. Such initiatives cannot be fostered by insincere efforts like terming "weakness" as "areas for improvement."

The Skanda Puran states, "In the nurturing of strengths lies the seed of greatness." We can unlock the potential for greatness within individuals and communities by fostering a strength-based culture.

Conclusion

In conclusion, focusing on the strengths of individuals is a powerful strategy for enhancing personal satisfaction, organisational success, and societal well-being. We can create environments that foster confidence, motivation, and innovation by recognising and leveraging what people do best. Conversely, an undue focus on weaknesses can be destructive, eroding self-esteem and hampering growth. Therefore, let us commit to building a culture that celebrates strengths, thereby enabling individuals to thrive and contribute positively to the world around them. As the Purans remind us, in nurturing strengths, we embrace the divine potential within each of us, paving the way for a brighter and more harmonious future.

About the Author

Partha Majumdar's leadership in the dynamic realm of software solutions is about technical prowess, strategic insight, and a unique style that blends these qualities with a personal touch. This makes his approach to innovation, efficiency, and business success unique.

His educational journey, which spans a Global Doctor of Business Administration to specialisations in Computational Data Sciences and Cybersecurity, reflects a commitment to continuous learning.

Majumdar's professional journey has been nothing short of extraordinary. As the Vice President of Software Engineering at J.P. Morgan Chase and Co. in his last role, he has spearheaded impactful initiatives, contributing to the evolution of software development paradigms. He is in the inception phase of starting his firm in the UAE and pursuing his PhD in Computer Science from Kalinga University. His earlier role as the Managing Director of Majumdar Consultancy Private Limited showcased his entrepreneurial spirit, where he successfully nurtured a fledgling business into a success with a global footprint.

Partha Majumdar's diverse talents and expertise are not confined to a single domain. His proficiency in software development, predictive modelling, descriptive data analysis, and Agile Project Management is a testament to his versatility, adaptability, and ability to deliver innovative solutions across various contexts.

Beyond his roles in corporate leadership, Majumdar has been recognised with numerous awards, including the "Excellence Award," "Gratitude Award," "Merit Award," and "Best IT Manager," underscoring his impact and leadership in the field. His commitment to excellence is further demonstrated through a comprehensive list of professional upskilling, covering project management, IT service management, and specialised areas like data science and cloud computing.

Majumdar's publications and patent attempts showcase a commitment to advancing the field. He has published twenty-one books on academia and knowledge dissemination, and his upcoming books and publications illustrate his dedication to sharing knowledge and insights.

In conclusion, Partha Majumdar's career is a testament to his multifaceted expertise, from spearheading successful ventures to influencing software development paradigms at industry giants. His unwavering commitment to innovation, coupled with a rich educational background and many certificates, positions him as a distinguished leader poised to continue making impactful contributions in the ever-evolving landscape of software solutions.

Books by the Author

Mastering Classification Algorithms for Machine Learning

This book explores the fundamentals of machine learning through classification algorithms, which are crucial for categorising inputs in applications like spam detection and fraud prevention. It covers problem-solving in machine learning, delving into Naïve Bayes, Logistic Regression (including the sigmoid function), Decision Trees (focusing on Gini Factor and Entropy), Random Forest, and Boosting techniques, providing a comprehensive guide to mastering classification challenges.

Link in Amazon Store: https://www.amazon.in/dp/935551851X

Neural Networks for Engineers

This book offers a comprehensive guide to neural networks, from foundational concepts to advanced deep learning techniques. This book bridges the gap between theory and application, covering Perceptrons, CNNs, RNNs, and more, with hands-on examples using Scikit-Learn, Keras, and PyTorch. Designed for engineers and practitioners, it demystifies neural network computations. It provides practical insights into deploying sophisticated models in real-world scenarios, making it an essential resource for mastering neural networks.

Link in Amazon Store: https://www.amazon.in/dp/B0DFVPV8YH

Machine Learning for Managers

This book is a comprehensive guide tailored for leaders aiming to leverage machine learning (ML) within their organisations. It simplifies ML concepts, emphasising strategic applications over technical complexity. The book covers integrating ML into business practices, ethical data use, and real-world industry applications, showcasing ML's role in enhancing operations and innovation. It also provides insights on team building in the ML era, promoting cross-disciplinary collaboration for effective ML adoption. This book is a strategic roadmap for managers to harness ML, driving informed decision-making and positioning their organisations for future success in an AI-driven landscape.

Link in Amazon Store: https://www.amazon.in/dp/B0CZ5XTQ1L

Deep Learning for Managers

This book is a pivotal guide for modern leaders navigating the AI revolution. It demystifies deep learning, making it accessible to managers without requiring deep technical knowledge. This book equips leaders with the insights to harness AI effectively, covering everything from the basics of artificial neural networks to the ethical considerations of AI deployment. It's an indispensable resource for any leader aiming to leverage deep learning as a strategic asset in today's rapidly evolving business landscape.

Link in Amazon Store: https://www.amazon.in/dp/B0CWDPWSN8

Generative AI for Managers

This book is a cutting-edge guide that demystifies Generative AI for business leaders eager to harness this technology for growth and innovation. It delves into how Generative AI can revolutionise aspects of business, from enhancing customer experiences to optimising operations and driving strategic decision-making. The book provides a wealth of practical applications, showcases how mundane tasks can be automated for efficiency, and presents strategies for fostering a culture of innovation through AI. Additionally, it offers guidance on the ethical implementation of AI technologies, ensuring they complement and augment human capabilities within the organisational framework, thereby paving the way for a future rich in opportunities and advancements.

Link in Amazon Store: https://www.amazon.in/dp/B0CXYBFJHD

ChatGPT AI for Managers

This book is a vital resource for leaders navigating the AI revolution, focusing on integrating Generative AI, like ChatGPT, in enhancing managerial functions and team dynamics. It provides practical insights into leveraging ChatGPT to streamline tasks, bolster decision-making, and encourage innovative thinking within teams. This guide transcends theoretical knowledge, offering actionable strategies for managers to complement their skills with AI, thereby elevating their leadership effectiveness. Through real-world applications and expert advice, readers will learn to harmonise traditional management with AI advancements, ensuring they remain at the forefront of the evolving business environment.

Link in Amazon Store: https://www.amazon.in/dp/B0CY8L4CQ9

Data Lakes for Managers

This book is a guide tailored for managers, detailing how to utilise data lakes effectively. It simplifies complex concepts and focuses on practical strategies and the strategic use of data lake technologies like AWS, Azure, and GCP. The book addresses common challenges such as data silos and security. It offers insights into the future of data technologies, empowering managers to harness data for strategic decision-making and innovation.

Link in Amazon Store:
https://www.amazon.in/dp/B0D35RCDPD

Recommendation Systems for Managers

This book demystifies the complexities of data-driven recommendation systems in an easy-to-understand format tailored for managers. This insightful guide traverses Time Series and Market Basket Analysis, AI, ML, and emerging technologies, offering a practical roadmap for implementing these systems. It's an indispensable resource for managers aiming to harness recommendation systems for strategic business decisions in the digital age.

Link in Amazon Store:
https://www.amazon.in/dp/B0CXNNSJRC

Learn Emotion Analysis with R

This book is a comprehensive guide to Emotion Analysis using Lexicons, offering a step-by-step code walkthrough for developing Sentiment and Emotion Analysis systems with data from WhatsApp and Twitter. It introduces R and Shiny programming, which is essential for building emotion analysis systems. The discussion then extends to the fundamentals of Sentiment and Emotion Analysis, leading to the creation of Shiny applications tailored for this purpose. The book concludes by developing a specialised tool for analysing emotions from Twitter and WhatsApp data. Additionally, it hints at advancing into Machine Learning for Emotion Analysis, contingent on the availability of labelled data, positioning this as a subsequent step for readers.

Link in Amazon Store: https://www.amazon.com/dp/B096K2SVF2

Starting a New AI Business

This book is a comprehensive guide designed for entrepreneurs looking to harness the power of artificial intelligence to build successful enterprises. Covering everything from defining business purpose and understanding AI fundamentals to exploring innovative business models and identifying market opportunities, this book provides practical insights and strategic guidance. With case studies of industry giants and lessons from ancient wisdom, it equips readers with the tools and knowledge to navigate the AI landscape effectively and achieve sustainable growth.

Link in Amazon Store: https://www.amazon.in/dp/B0CL3YBSF8

Ten Essays on AI

This book offers a deep dive into the world of artificial intelligence, covering critical topics such as data-analytic thinking, data quality, AI strategies, and the evolution of AI technology. This comprehensive collection provides readers with practical insights and theoretical knowledge to harness AI's potential and navigate its challenges effectively.

Link in Amazon Store: https://www.amazon.in/dp/B0D9PMJBWB

Essays on Machine Learning

This book is a concise and practical guide for managers and business leaders seeking to understand and apply machine learning in their organisations. This book distils complex concepts into clear, accessible insights, covering foundational principles, practical applications, and advanced techniques. Designed as a ready reckoner, it empowers non-technical leaders with the knowledge to make informed decisions in the AI-driven landscape, driving innovation and strategic growth.

Link in Amazon Store: https://www.amazon.in/dp/B0DDHZ78Z7

Linear Programming for Project Management Professionals

This guide provides project management professionals with

strategies for project crashing using linear programming, ensuring timely completion and cost efficiency. It introduces basic project management concepts, monitoring techniques, and linear programming problem formulation. The book explains how to solve these problems using Microsoft Excel's Solver and applying time and cost optimisation methods to real-world scenarios. It equips project management teams with a comprehensive toolkit to handle complex challenges effectively.

Link in Amazon Store: https://www.amazon.com/dp/B09PD1GFMY

Gartner Research Analysis

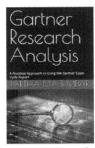
The book provides a clear framework for leveraging insights from the Gartner Hype-Cycle Report, an essential resource for understanding technological trends. It simplifies identifying and evaluating emerging technologies, their developers, and market readiness. A live case study illustrates practical application while emphasising the need for comprehensive research beyond the report. Essential for those seeking strategic technological guidance, this book demystifies the complex data presented in the Gartner Hype Cycle.

Link in Amazon Store: https://www.amazon.com/dp/B0CK582Y2M

Corporate Lessons I Learned

This book encapsulates 34 years of corporate experiences up to 2023, presenting a collection of impactful incidents and interactions that shaped the author's career. Primarily aimed at middle and lower-level managers, it offers humorous and insightful recollections that serve as practical guidelines for navigating daily challenges in the corporate world. The author illustrates valuable lessons learned through various encounters, making it a helpful resource for understanding and excelling in corporate management.

Link in Amazon Store: https://www.amazon.in/dp/B0CL3YBSF8

Rise and Fall

This book follows Mahesh Roy's transformation from a small-town boy to a powerful hotelier entangled in illegal activities. Driven by ambition, Mahesh's world unravels as he confronts the consequences of his choices. In a parallel narrative, lawyer Durga Varma fights to expose the truth behind the mysterious death of her beloved Raj in Mahesh's casino. This gripping novel explores the themes of power, greed, justice, and redemption in a dramatic clash between integrity and corruption.

Link in Amazon Store: https://www.amazon.in/dp/B0DFY5F3VF

Transformation

This book tells the story of Roopesh, a successful yet deeply troubled man who embarks on a journey of change guided by Vedant, a mentor versed in ancient wisdom. Through small, deliberate steps, Roopesh learns to reclaim his life, face his inner demons, and find balance in the everyday. The book explores self-discipline, mindfulness, and the importance of surrendering control, offering a powerful reminder that true transformation begins within and that it's never too late to change.

Link in Amazon Store: https://www.amazon.in/dp/B0DGG5343N

Mutual Fund Investing

This book is a comprehensive guide for middle-class investors in India, simplifying mutual funds. It covers types of mutual funds, differences between open-ended and closed funds, systematic investments, tax implications, and risk assessment. It also teaches advanced techniques like Piotrowski's F-Score and Mohanram's G-Score for building diversified portfolios and evaluating fund performance. Suitable for beginners and seasoned investors, it is essential for achieving financial growth and security through mutual funds.

Link in Amazon Store: https://www.amazon.com/dp/B0CYNG6B12

Creating an Investment Portfolio

This book delves into the scientific process of making informed investment decisions, highlighting the importance for individuals and corporations. It explores critical theories and applications in portfolio creation, covering various investment vehicles like fixed deposits, mutual funds, and shares, emphasising the necessary mathematics. Additionally, it introduces simple yet widely used tools for investment calculations. Designed to be accessible to a broad audience, this book is an invaluable guide for beginners and experienced investors aiming to enhance their understanding and effectiveness in investing.

Link in Amazon Store: https://www.amazon.com/dp/B0CK99SPKZ

Essay on the Indian Knowledge System – Part 1

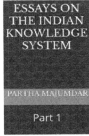

The book delves into the Indian Knowledge System (IKS), a comprehensive approach to compiling, conserving, and disseminating India's rich knowledge heritage across various disciplines such as science, mathematics, social sciences, medicine, philosophy, art, and spirituality. It highlights the global perspective of IKS and its relevance in sharing India's intellectual legacy with the world. The study of Indology, or "Bharatatattva," as it's known in Indian scholarship, further explores the historical, cultural, linguistic, and literary facets of the Indian subcontinent. Through a series of concise essays, this book, one of a trilogy on ancient India, offers insights into Bharatatattva, underscoring India's significant contributions to global knowledge.

Link in Amazon Store: https://www.amazon.com/dp/B0CXNN95TR

Essay on the Indian Knowledge System – Part 2

This book explores ancient India's profound contributions to various scientific disciplines, such as mathematics, astronomy, medicine, and metallurgy. It highlights India's enduring influence on global scientific thought by examining the works of great scholars like Aryabhata and Sushruta. With a unique blend of philosophy and empirical science, this book offers insights into how ancient wisdom continues to shape modern scientific inquiry. It is an essential read for those interested in the history of science.

Link in Amazon Store: https://www.amazon.in/dp/B0DJ7NZH82

Good People Are Tested the Most

This book explores the lives of seven extraordinary individuals who faced immense challenges and emerged victorious. The book delves into resilience, faith, and the triumph of the human spirit, featuring Bhakt Prahalad, Raja Harishchandra, Lord Shri Ram, Arjun, Hercules, Swami Vivekananda, and Sardar Milkha Singh. Their inspiring stories highlight the importance of maintaining principles, overcoming significant challenges, and the ultimate triumph of good over evil, serving as inspiration for all.

Link in Amazon Store: https://www.amazon.in/dp/B0D1FM44H9

Sailing through the Kali Yug

This book explores the relevance of ancient Indian scriptures, especially the Purans, in understanding the complexities of the present age. It introduces the concept of Yugs, highlighting Rishi Krishna Dwaipayan Ved Vyas's role and the Purans' structure. The book details the moral decline of the Kali Yug, starting from Raja Parikshit's reign, and emphasises Dharam's four pillars. It promotes Bhakti and practical spiritual practices as pathways to maintaining integrity and achieving liberation.

Link in Amazon Store:
https://www.amazon.in/dp/B0D6M34JCT

The Maha Purans in Brief

 This book distils the essence of eighteen ancient Vedic scriptures, offering insights into their themes, stories, and teachings. The book explores the relevance of Puranic wisdom in modern life, providing guidance on ethics, leadership, environmental sustainability, and personal development. It serves as an accessible guide to understanding the rich spiritual heritage of Indian culture and applying its timeless lessons to contemporary challenges.

Link in Amazon Store:
https://www.amazon.in/dp/B0CW8GJ22L

Weekend in Jordan

Thanks to the country's visa-on-arrival policy for Indians, the authors spontaneously travelled to Jordan to celebrate their 20th wedding anniversary. Their weekend was filled with memorable experiences, from Petra's historical wonders to the Dead Sea's unique allure and Amman's vibrant city life. Despite its modest size, Jordan's rich offerings left a lasting impression. This book recounts their remarkable journey, providing insights into the treasures of Jordan.

Link in Amazon Store:
https://www.amazon.com/dp/B0CK5N6B3W

Elephant Ride in Chang Wangpo

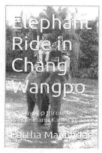

In 2022, Thailand saw a significant influx of approximately 11.5 million tourists, underlining tourism's vital role in its economy, contributing around 6% to the Thai GDP. Reflecting on their past residency in Bangkok from 1996 to 1999, the authors seized a chance to revisit Thailand in 2018, noticing considerable changes. An efficient metro system has alleviated the once notorious Bangkok traffic, enhancing city navigation. While many cherished aspects remained, improvements in the road network and increased attractions enriched their experience. Coinciding with their 26th wedding anniversary, the business trip also included leisure exploration in Bangkok and Kanchanaburi, with a memorable visit to Chang Wangpo, blending nostalgia, discovery, and celebration.

Link in Amazon Store: https://www.amazon.com/dp/B0CKGWH97S

Weekend in South Sikkim

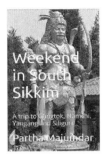

This book explores the less-travelled South Sikkim, diverging from popular tourist spots like Gangtok and Nathu La Pass. It covers captivating destinations such as Tsomgo Lake, Baba Ka Mandir, and Temi Tea Gardens. The authors delve into the cultural and spiritual essence of South Sikkim with visits to Namchi's Char Dham and Samdruptse Monastery. The narrative also extends to Yangang and the Bengal Safari in Siliguri, West Bengal, offering a comprehensive travelogue with diverse experiences.

Link in Amazon Store:
https://www.amazon.com/dp/B0CKL1DNTJ

Trips to Dubai

This travelogue unveils the multifaceted allure of Dubai, a top-tier tourist hub known for landmarks like the Burj Khalifa and Burj Al Arab, alongside thrilling experiences such as helicopter rides and dolphin encounters at the Atlantis. It extends beyond Dubai, shedding light on Abu Dhabi and Sharjah attractions, like the adrenaline-pumping Ferrari World and the enchanting Desert Safari. The author shares personal adventures, offering insights into the intricacies of visiting Dubai and navigating the Gulf region, making this book a valuable resource for anyone looking to explore the rich experiences Dubai and its neighbouring emirates offer.

Link in Amazon Store: https://www.amazon.com/dp/B0CKRYQKDN

1-Day Trips from Bengaluru

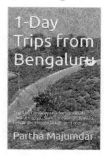

From 1975 to 2023, Bengaluru evolved from a retirees' haven to India's Silicon Valley, also renowned as Garden City. While Bengaluru has numerous tourist attractions and activity hubs, the city's vicinity offers many exploration destinations. This book focuses on day-trip-worthy spots around Bengaluru, places steeped in historical significance. It does not cover prominent cities like Mysuru, Chennai, and Hyderabad, as well as scenic locales like Ooty, Goa, and Kerala, as they need more than a day to tour.

Link in Amazon Store: . https://www.amazon.com/dp/B0CLK58KTB

A Trip to the Wagah Border

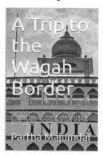

The Wagah Border, straddling India and Pakistan near Amritsar and Lahore, is famed for its ceremonial displays by border forces, symbolising hope amidst strained relations. This checkpoint, pivotal for prisoner exchanges, represents a unique reconciliation potential. On festive occasions, friendly exchanges between the forces foster harmony. The book visually explores Chandigarh, Shimla, Amritsar, and the Wagah Border, highlighting their rich cultures and historical importance.

Link in Amazon Store: https://www.amazon.com/dp/B0CLYTQ6PV

Weekend Getaways from Bengaluru

This guidebook enhances the tourism experience in India, emphasising the country's improved accessibility and facilities that cater to all traveller categories. It explicitly outlines short trips from Bengaluru, covering a mix of destinations accessible by road, rail, and air. The book is a resource for planning 2-, 3-, and 4-day excursions to various South Indian locales and select sites in Maharashtra, featuring popular tourist destinations such as Ooty, Kodaikanal, and Mysuru, as well as revered places of worship like Kukke Subramanya and Dharamsthala. It offers practical travel tips, what to anticipate on journeys and insights into each destination's unique offerings.

Link in Amazon Store: https://www.amazon.com/dp/B0CMNRKWQ9